The Joslyns of Lynhurst

The Joslyns of Lynhurst

✦

The True Story of George, Sarah, and Their Castle

Daniel Kiper

iUniverse, Inc.

New York Lincoln Shanghai

The Joslyns of Lynhurst
The True Story of George, Sarah, and Their Castle

iUniverse books may be ordered through booksellers or by contacting:

iUniverse
2021 Pine Lake Road, Suite 100
Lincoln, NE 68512
www.iuniverse.com
1-800-Authors (1-800-288-4677)

Cover Photograph: This photograph, circa 1890, depicts George and Sarah Joslyn mounted on their horses under the watchful eyes of one of their champion St. Bernard dogs. The photograph was probably taken at the entrance of the Grand Union Hotel in Saratoga Springs, New York (Photograph from the Joslyn Art Museum Library).

ISBN-13: 978-0-595-38576-8 (pbk)
ISBN-13: 978-0-595-82955-2 (ebk)
ISBN-10: 0-595-38576-1 (pbk)
ISBN-10: 0-595-82955-4 (ebk)

Printed in the United States of America

Contents

Acknowledgments vii

Preface ix

Introduction xi

Chapter 1:   The Early Years to Empire (1848–1880) 1

Chapter 2:   Omaha (1880–1892) 8

Chapter 3:   The Grounds of Lynhurst (1893–1897) 15

Chapter 4:   Building the Castle of Lynhurst (1898–1903) 23

Chapter 5:   The Interior of Lynhurst Castle (1903–1904) 51

Chapter 6:   Self-Imposed Exile (1904–1906) 87

Chapter 7:   The Social Whirl (1907–1912) 96

Chapter 8:   Beginnings and Endings (1913–1916) 103

Chapter 9:   Building George's Memorial (1917–1931) 112

Chapter 10: Sarah's Legacy (1932–1940) 130

Epilogue (1940–2006) 135

Chapter Notes 137

Index 159

Acknowledgments

This work would not have been possible without the assistance and contributions of these individuals and organizations: my wife, Pam Scott; the Omaha Public Library and their excellent collection of early Omaha newspapers; Joanne Ferguson Cavanaugh, Lynn Sullivan, and the staff of the W. Dale Clark Library; Christine Dahlin and Jo Grebenick of the Joslyn Castle Institute; the Friends of Joslyn Castle; the Joslyn Art Museum; Lynn Meyer and the City of Omaha Planning Department; the Douglas County Historical Society; the Nebraska State Historical Society; Vern Lenzen and the Durham Western Heritage Museum; the Omaha World-Herald Library-Link; the Church of Jesus Christ of the Latter-Day Saints; Stephen Sylvester of Hollywood Heritage; Lyndhurst on the Hudson; Lannie McNichols; and finally, Sarah Watson, Patricia Kiper-Rummer, and Annette Huff, for their invaluable help in editing the manuscript.

Preface

In the spring of 1998, a friend asked me whether I would be interested in becoming a docent for the Friends of Joslyn Castle (FOJC). The FOJC was a recently formed organization dedicated to preserving and restoring the Joslyn Castle in Omaha, Nebraska. She invited me to come to an organizational meeting for new docents at the castle. I agreed to go because I had never seen the inside of the structure, and I thought this would be an excellent opportunity to do so.

I was awestruck. I soon became a devoted docent and tour guide. From 1999 until 2004, I served on the board of the FOJC and became involved in researching the history of the Joslyns and their estate. I was dismayed at how little information existed, and I was appalled that much of it proved to be incorrect on closer examination. I wanted to know the real story, and in early 2004, I embarked on a two-year research project to discover the truth.

I was not alone in this desire to know more. Each year, thousands of people visit the Joslyn Castle. Many visitors are similarly awed by the opulent castle and impressed by the estate's spacious grounds. They want more information about the estate and the people who built it. Until now, there has been no comprehensive or accurate way to satisfy their needs. This is unfortunate because the Joslyn Castle is a significant architectural structure. The unique castle is perhaps the finest example of Scottish Baronial architecture in the United States. The beautifully carved stone exterior and the lavish interiors offer a glimpse into an era of fine craftsmanship and beautifully executed design. The home's exotic hardwood paneling, elegant art-glass windows, intricate tiling, and plasterwork are some of the finest examples of their type. Several nationally renowned architects, designers, and artisans were involved in creating the grounds of the estate and building its castle.

The story of the couple who built the estate is equally compelling. The tale of George and Sarah Joslyn is the stuff of pure Americana. It is a rags-to-riches tale of a young couple who came West to make their fortune and who succeeded beyond their wildest expectations, leaving behind a vast media empire and a magnificent memorial dedicated to the arts. I hope you will find their story fascinating and come away with an appreciation of how much these amazing people achieved for their adopted city of Omaha.

Introduction

There is no way to know exactly when and how George and Sarah arrived in Omaha. They are first listed as residents of Omaha in the 1880 census, conducted in the late spring and early summer of that year. The most plausible scenario was that they came to Omaha by train. It is easy to imagine the young couple stepping down from a train onto the wooden platform of the Omaha station on a sunny spring day. They had come from Montreal via Des Moines to start a new life in Omaha. Omaha was then a rapidly growing city, which in the span of twenty-six years, had grown to a population of over thirty thousand. The two had brought little with them. In later years, George would claim the couple had gone to Des Moines to look for work and had arrived there with only "nine dollars and a satchel of old, but serviceable clothing."[1]

This was perhaps an exaggeration of their circumstances, but they were a couple of modest means. In their first year in Omaha, they slept above the company's offices in a small room filled with the smells of printer's ink and damp paper stock. They did not stay there long. Within ten years, George controlled the company, and they lived in a large house on the western edge of the city. At the time of his death, he had amassed one of the largest fortunes in Nebraska, and the couple lived in a massive castle at their estate of Lynhurst on a ridge overlooking the city. (Lynhurst is the name that George gave his estate, and he reportedly hated people referring to it as the Joslyns' castle.)

They also took an interest in their community. They gave generously of their time and money. They would donate land or money to help build a university, a community playhouse, and homes to care for the elderly, children, and animals. Sarah would fund a stunning art museum in memory of her husband, still a crown jewel amid Omaha's cultural treasures. In the end, they left their home and the bulk of their fortune to charitable causes.

Sadly, George and Sarah are almost forgotten now. They and their accomplishments are lost amid the exaggerated stories and rumors told about them. Current accounts stress the more sensational aspects of their lives. In some cases, these stories have no apparent factual basis. Most of these exaggerations are harmless. However, two myths about the couple are so ugly and have become so pervasive that they should be discussed.

The first is George's ownership of the Cook Remedy Company. Cook Remedy was a small company that marketed a patent medicine called "Our Magic Remedy" from 1888 until 1908. It was a supposed cure for a sexually transmitted disease. The firm was a very small and insignificant part of George's business empire, but stories told about it have assumed mythological proportions, implying the firm was the foundation of his wealth. In truth, it appears that George's major reason for owning the firm was to provide employment for his brother and later his niece's husband. His name is also unfairly associated with another patent medicine called "Big G," which was sold by the Evans Chemical Company of Cincinnati, Ohio, a firm he was never involved with.[2]

The second part of the Joslyn story that is exaggerated is the purportedly eccentric behavior of Sarah Joslyn. Current mythology portrays Sarah as disconnected from reality, forgetful, and aloof to the point of rudeness. Furthermore, many who write about her insinuate that fellow socialites shunned her, and that she spent her time as a recluse. Finally, the myths imply that she was miserly, and that after her husband's death she hoarded her vast fortune, dressing in old, worn clothing, and living like an impoverished hermit. Researching Sarah Joslyn's life demonstrates clearly that these stories are baseless.

1

The Early Years to Empire
(1848–1880)

Joslin or Joslyn

Before beginning this section, it is necessary to explain the different spellings of the name Joslyn. When George was born, his family spelled their last name Joslin. George and Sarah continued to spell their surname this way until they arrived in Omaha. Shortly after their arrival, they changed the spelling of their name to Joslyn. The change in spelling was reportedly due to a batch of misspelled business cards, which had George's last name spelled Joslyn. He is said to have liked the new spelling and adopted it. An alternative version has Sarah suggesting the change in spelling.[1] What we do know is that the change occurred in 1882. Other members of the family continued to spell their name Joslin. In this text, the preferred spelling of each individual is used.

Waitsfield, Vermont

In 1800, twenty-four-year-old Joseph Joslin married Betsy Chamberlain. The new couple moved to the town of Waitsfield, located in central Vermont. General Benjamin Wait had established Waitsfield in 1789. It is located in Washington County, in the thickly forested Mad River Valley, an area of verdant hills and low, rock-strewn mountains. Today the town and surrounding area are popular tourist destinations for winter skiing and autumn bus tours, where tourists come to admire the brilliant colors of the foliage. In 1800, the area was a collection of small farms. After their arrival, Joseph bought a farm, and the couple settled into their new home.

Joseph and Betsy had four children before Betsy's death in 1807. In 1808, Joseph married a woman named Nancy. (Her last name may have been Spalding.) He and Nancy had three daughters before she died in 1813. Their second daughter, Calista, was born on February 13, 1810.[2] She would later marry James Selleck of nearby Fayston, and they would have five children. Their youngest daughter was born on April 14, 1851, or perhaps April 14, 1853; the exact date is unclear. They named her Sarah Hannah Selleck.[3] Joseph would marry one final time after Nancy's death. On July 8, 1817, he wed Abigail Taylor. They had five children. Alfred, their youngest son, was born on August 23, 1822.[4]

Alfred married Ester Ann Rice in 1847. After their marriage, the couple moved to Lowell, Massachusetts, for a brief period. In Lowell, their first child was born on June 30, 1848, a son they named George Alfred Joslin.[5] The first years were difficult for George. The 1850 census listed George's mother as still living with her parents.[6] Although two-year-old George was not listed as a resident of the house, it is unlikely he was not with his mother. This may indicate that Alfred had found it difficult to make a living in Lowell and had sent his wife and young son back to Waitsfield. Soon after 1850, Alfred returned to Waitsfield and started a farm.

As a young man, George worked on his father's farm and attended the local school. At the time, the highest level of education available in Waitsfield was a two-year high school that recently had been constructed in the town.[7] It is unclear whether George received any education beyond this. He disliked working on the farm and, at an early age, decided to leave home and look for other work.

It is not surprising that George preferred leaving home to working on his father's farm. Farming in central Vermont was an arduous occupation. The ground is hilly and the soil riddled with large rocks. This made farming a very labor-intensive operation, which limited the size of the farms in Vermont. As settlers began farming in the central United States, the flatter terrain and better soil allowed for larger and more efficient operations. The financial problems faced by Waitsfield's farmers intensified with the introduction of technological innovations, such as the mechanical reaper and better plows. These devices greatly increased efficiency and reduced production costs for the large Midwestern farms. Conversely, plows and reapers did not work well in the soil of Vermont, and they were expensive to buy. Their cost put them beyond the reach of most small farmers. This inability to compete effectively led most farmers in New England to abandon farming. This trend would have a disastrous effect on Waitsfield and central Vermont.

When George was born, Waitsfield had a population of slightly over one thousand people. During the next seventy years, the town's population would steadily decline until its population reached 682 in 1920. It was only after tourism rescued the local economy in the 1960s that the town's population began to rebound.[8] Prior to the growth of tourism, there were few other economic opportunities for ambitious young people.

Although George and Sarah had been born in an isolated area of the country, national events would do much to shape their lives and futures. Since the beginning of the United States, two forces had competed to shape the nation. One of these was the concept of manifest destiny, the belief that it was the destiny of the United States to expand its territory until it controlled the entire continent. The second force was the issue of slavery. The conflict between the desire to control more territory and efforts to limit or abolish slavery dominated political debate in the United States until the mid-nineteenth century. On several occasions, political compromises narrowly averted the dissolution of the United States.

In 1854, passage of the Kansas-Nebraska Act dealt a near-fatal blow to this delicately crafted balance. This act undid earlier compromises and allowed future states to decide the question of allowing slavery themselves. The situation was further inflamed in 1856 by the infamous *Dred Scott* decision. The U.S. Supreme Court decided that Scott (who was a slave) was not a citizen and could not sue for his freedom. In its decision, the Court also declared that the 1820 Missouri Compromise Act was unconstitutional and that the U.S. Congress could not restrict slavery. This effectively made any additional rapprochement impossible. These events fueled the growing antagonism between the industrialized and free Northern states and the agricultural and slaveholding Southern states.

After Abraham Lincoln was elected president of the United States in 1860 without winning a single Southern state, the situation rapidly disintegrated. After Lincoln's election, eleven Southern states seceded from the nation, beginning with South Carolina on December 20, 1860. This led to the outbreak of the Civil War on April 12, 1861. The war lasted until the Confederate Army finally surrendered on April 9, 1865.

The war ended with a bitterly divided nation that had undergone a wrenching transformation. The country had gone from a nation with a predominantly agrarian economy to one with an economy based more on urban industry and commerce. The war had dislodged vast segments of the population from their homes, and over 600,000 young men had died during the war. The need for workers during the war and the questions it raised about personal rights had changed the role of women in the country, accelerating the women's suffrage movement. The railway system and transportation infrastructure had greatly expanded, allowing the population greater opportunities for travel and commerce. The Civil War was a high price to pay, but the conflict remade the United States.

Events related to the Civil War would profoundly affect the life of George Joslyn. During the war, oftentimes, the entire population of young men in a community would serve in the same unit during the fighting. The families and friends they left behind had a keen desire to follow the course of the war and keep abreast of their hometown unit's progress and well-being. This demand for information about events occurring on the battlefields and in other parts of the nation greatly increased the public's interest in national news. At the same time, the demand for men to fight in the war rapidly depleted the ranks of experienced printers, making it difficult for smaller newspapers to meet this growing demand. The increase in the number of newspapers, and the shrinking ranks of printers, provided a perfect opportunity for the auxiliary printing industry to thrive. It was in this industry that George would later make his fortune.

Soon after George finished school, he left Waitsfield to seek his fortune in Montreal. One obituary written about him indicated that he arrived in Montreal when he was fifteen. It reported that his first job there had been selling newspapers on trains.[9] By 1872, George had taken a job with the Rice Brothers' Paper Company in Montreal, a firm that his uncles, Walter and George Rice, had started.[10] The company manufactured paper shirt collars, a popular product at the time. Inexpensive to produce, they were discarded after use, which eliminated the need to wash the entire shirt when only the collar was soiled. The use of these detachable collars later spawned the term "white-collar" worker.[11] The Rice brothers decided to expand into the printing industry, and George transferred to their new company.[12]

Three years earlier, George had returned to Vermont and married Sarah on September 28, 1872. It is unclear how they met. Sarah's obituary mentions that she had moved to Waitsfield to live with her aunt.[13] If this is true, given the small size of the town, there would have been many opportunities for them to have met. After their marriage, Sarah moved with George to Montreal, where he continued to work at Rice Brothers. Shortly after they arrived, their lives were marred by tragedy, when their only son, Clifton Howard, died soon after his birth in 1873.[14] George continued working for his uncles until 1879, when he left to accept a job offer from the Iowa Printing Company in Des Moines.

Creating the Joslyn Empire

In 1872, an influential group of Iowa newspaper reporters and politicians started the State Printing Company. The firm went through several changes of name, direction, and ownership. First formed as a combined newspaper and printing house, the firm finally settled on the auxiliary printing business and was renamed the Iowa Printing Company. In 1876, two young men from Vermont, Walter E. Andrews and William H. Welsh, bought the company. Andrews had begun working for the *Iowa State Leader*, a local newspaper in Des Moines, in 1872.[15] In 1876, he began managing Iowa Printing, and soon thereafter, he and Welsh bought the company. In 1879, they merged with an auxiliary printer in Kansas City and decided to open an office in Omaha called the Omaha Newspaper Union. Ultimately, George Joslyn became manager of the new branch.[16]

Although George later maintained that he had arrived in Des Moines without a job, it strains belief that he and Sarah would travel over a thousand miles to look for work. In spite of his later statements, it is quite possible that Andrews or Welsh, or both, knew George from Vermont and offered him the job before he came West. Barre, the city where Andrews attended college, is located less than fifty miles from Waitsfield.[17] Regardless of why the couple came to Des Moines, they did not stay long, and by the spring of 1880, George and Sarah were in Omaha.

The auxiliary printing industry dates back to an experiment conducted by Moses Beach in 1841. Beach acquired a copy of President John Tyler's annual state of the union message to Congress. He printed several copies of the message, using the same typeface, for twelve other newspapers, changing only the sheet's masthead for each paper. (A masthead is the title of a newspaper.) This allowed all the papers to carry Tyler's message without each publisher having to set the type for it.[18] After this initial ready-print experiment, the industry experienced slow and uneven growth until 1861. With the beginning of the Civil War, and the subsequent demand for news it generated, the auxiliary printing industry began a period of rapid growth that would continue into the early twentieth century.

The auxiliary printing industry met this demand with a product called "ready print," a standard-page-sized newspaper partially preprinted with advertisements, national and international news, and a variety of other features on the inside pages. The outside pages were left blank. (While this was the original format, later the industry offered ready-print sheets in a variety of formats.)[19] Small newspapers printed local news and advertisements on the blank pages. The preprinted material covering the war and news from around the country allowed the readers of these newspapers to follow the events that were affecting their family and friends who had moved away or were fighting in the war. The inclusion of advertising allowed auxiliary printers to offer their product at a cost that rivaled that of blank newsprint. In the latter part of the nineteenth century, the economies of "ready printing" allowed both small newspapers and the auxiliary printing industry to flourish.

Auxiliary printers also provided other types of content. In 1871, the A. N. Kellogg Company of Chicago introduced the first continued story, or serialization, into an auxiliary publication.[19] Serials were popular with both readers and newspaper publishers. The auxiliary houses would publish the stories in sections, usually a short chapter each week. The most successful stories would have unresolved or cliffhanger endings at the end of each section, leaving readers anxious for the next installment. Several notable authors such as Stephen Crane, Edgar Allen Poe, Louisa May Alcott, Charles Dickens, and Jack London wrote serialized stories.

As technology evolved, the auxiliary printing industry began to offer products in other formats, most notably stereotype. These inexpensive plates were etched with print matter in standard sizes; they made it easy for printers to compose their own newspaper pages. This is where the term "boilerplate" originated. While generally thought to refer to the standard printed content, the term was actually coined because one of the first manufacturers of stereotype plates shared a building with a stove company.[21] The plates were light and easily installed on printing presses. The use of stereotype allowed publishers even greater flexibility in composing the content of their newspapers. Instead of using the preprinted sheets, they could now choose individual news items and features that they felt would most interest their readers and compose their own pages.

Other products sold by the auxiliary printing industry were materials in the forms of mat and copy. Mat was a product similar to the stereotype plates, but because it was made of a cardboard-like paper, it cost less than metal stereotype plates. Copy, as the name implies, was material that newspapers could use without any printing services. These products allowed the industry to expand beyond small newspapers to offer products and services to mid-range and large metropolitan newspapers. The auxiliary printers also provided content in the form of illustrations, and later, photographs.

The industry continued to flourish until a series of changes in the United States led to its eventual demise. The first changes were advancements in printing technology that lessened small newspapers' reliance on the preprinted material. A second change was the steady movement of the population of the United States from small towns to large cities. This gradually eroded the smaller newspapers' markets, reducing the number of rural newspapers in the country, which were the major customers of the Western Newspaper Union (WNU). Finally, small newspapers faced increasing competition from larger newspapers. Due to reduced transportation costs, large newspapers were finding it more economical to ship their papers to small towns. As the number of smaller newspapers plummeted, the Western Newspaper Union also saw its fortunes fall. On March 29, 1952, the WNU shipped its last orders of ready print.[22] In 1961, Hammermill Paper Company purchased the company.[23] Today, what is left of George's company is part of the Xpedx Division of the International Paper Company.[24]

In 1936, Elmo Scott Watson wrote a history of newspaper syndicates. In his book he asserted, "Finally, in 1890 he (Joslyn) became president, general manager and principal stockholder, and from that time the Western Newspaper Union was George A. Joslyn and George A. Joslyn was the Western Newspaper Union."[25]

It would be just as correct to say that, by 1916, the auxiliary printing industry was George A. Joslyn, and George A. Joslyn was the auxiliary printing industry. George began as manager of the Omaha Newspaper Union in 1880, and within a few years was treasurer of the Western Newspaper Union. During the first ten years, the company expanded its operations through a series of acquisitions. In 1888, the WNU opened the Great Western Type Foundry in Omaha and expanded into the sale of printing equipment, newsprint, stock typefaces, electroplate, and stereotype plate. By 1890, the firm had offices or plants in Chicago, Dallas, Denver, Detroit, Des Moines, Lincoln, New York City, San Antonio, Topeka, Winfield (Kansas), and Omaha. The firm served 1,745 newspapers and had estimated annual sales exceeding $1 million. It consumed twenty-five carloads of newsprint a month. In 1890, George took control of the firm, became its major stockholder, and installed himself as president and general manager.[26]

Under George's leadership, the firm continued to grow by acquiring rival firms and opening new offices. In 1906, the WNU bought one of its largest rivals, the A. N. Kellogg Company, and added 1,827 newspaper customers. In 1909, the WNU took control of the Northwestern Newspaper Union. In 1910, the firm bought out the Chicago Newspaper Union, a bitter rival. Finally, after a protracted price war in 1912, the American Press Association, WNU's last real rival, requested permission from the federal government to sell its plate operations to the WNU.

Although the government initially blocked the sale as potentially violating antitrust laws, it later relented and allowed American Press to sell its plate operations to the WNU. The negotiations between the firms and the government were long and contentious, and the sale did not become final until 1917. This final merger gave the Western Newspaper Union a virtual monopoly of the auxiliary printing industry.[27]

At its height in 1923, the WNU had plants and offices in thirty-seven cities across the United States. Sadly, George did not live to see this final triumph. However, in thirty-six years he had managed to turn the small firm he started working for in 1880 (at a salary of $18 a week) into a massive media conglomerate with 14,273 customers (in 1923). It reached an estimated weekly audience of sixty million people at the time of his death.[28]

2

Omaha (1880–1892)

The Hotels

In addition to the WNU, George was involved in several other business ventures. Besides his ill-advised ownership of Cook Remedy, he founded the Western Chemical Company, which became the largest processor of lithium in the United States.[1] He also invested heavily in real estate, and owned six major buildings in Omaha at the time of his death. George and Sarah's most interesting business venture was their foray into hotel management. When George and Sarah arrived in Omaha, their first home was a room in the Western Newspaper Union building. In 1883, they moved from this location after George took control of two hotels in Omaha. He and Sarah lived in one of them until they moved to a home at 2522 Davenport in 1886.[2] Their first hotel was the St. Charles, located at 1208–10 Harney Street. The St. Charles was a residence hotel that charged its guests $4 per week.[3] This type of establishment operated as a larger version of a lodging house, a forerunner of modern apartment complexes. It provided inexpensive long-term accommodations.

The second hotel was the Metropolitan Hotel, located at 1122–24 Douglas Street, three blocks from the St. Charles. The Metropolitan catered to travelers staying in Omaha overnight or for a short period. It was considered one of the more upscale hotels in the city, advertising rates of $2 per night.[4]

A persistent rumor regarding the Joslyns and the Metropolitan concerns the role Sarah Joslyn played in the management of the hotel. Legend has it that she managed the hotel's restaurant and was renowned for her baking skills. Local people would flock to the hotel on Sundays to enjoy Sarah's pies. While it is not clear if the story about her baking skills is true, she does appear to have played a role in managing the hotel and its restaurant.

In a newspaper article, George gave Sarah most of the credit for the Metropolitan's success. Later in the article there was a more concrete description of her role, that "she is here publicly accorded large credit for success attending the hotel, not alone in a financial way, but for the reputation it secured for epicurean excellencies and home comforts, to those who make it their stopping place when in the metropolis of Nebraska."[5]

George ran the Metropolitan Hotel until late 1885 or early 1886, when control of the property passed to a partnership owned by G. M. Gay and John Hoar.[6] George operated the St. Charles for an additional year. Around this time, he began planning a new six-story hotel that he may have intended to name the Joslyn Hotel or the Hotel Joslyn. George chose a site bordered by Ninth and Tenth streets and Farnam and Harney streets. Excavation of the site began in 1887, but something went wrong, and construction of the hotel stopped. On July 26, 1890, the *Omaha Excelsior* reported that Walter Andrews of Des Moines, who was still president of the Western Newspaper Union in 1887, had stepped in with $50,000 to bail George out of the situation.[7] After failing to build his hotel, George abandoned the hotel business. By 1888, he and his wife were financially secure, and they did not need the additional income the hotels generated. In addition, George was poised to take control of the WNU, and he began to focus almost entirely on the printing business.

One final story related to the hotels was that George had purchased the Metropolitan so he could make additional money from WNU customers. When WNU customers would visit Omaha on business, George would arrange for them to stay at the Metropolitan. This allowed him to make a profit from his customers' business with the WNU and make additional money from their hotel bills. While some have scoffed at this idea, it may have some merit.

It is common practice for companies to enter into contracts with hotels to provide a reduced corporate rate for the company's employees or customers. In return, the company guarantees it will use the hotel exclusively. George was a farsighted and innovative businessman, and it is not hard to believe that he had this type of arrangement with WNU customers and vendors. They stayed with him at a discount, and he kept his hotel full.

Family and Friends

During this period, several individuals who were to play important roles in the lives of George and Sarah arrived in Omaha. Some were relatives from Vermont, and some were friends they met after their arrival in Omaha. The first relative who came to Omaha was George's cousin, Ferdinand R. Joslin. Ferdinand, or Ferd, was born in Waitsfield on April 20, 1849. He was the son of George's uncle, Almon Joslin, and his wife, Sarah.[8] George and Ferd grew up together in Waitsfield and remained close their entire lives. Ferdinand had remained in Waitsfield, where he lived with his parents. In 1881, the thirty-two-year-old Ferd moved to Omaha. The *1882–83 Omaha City Directory* listed Fred R. Joslin (Ferdinand's shortened name was almost always misspelled as Fred) as the manager of both the St. Charles and the Metropolitan hotels.[9]

Shortly after he arrived in Omaha, Ferdinand met Rose Matilda (Tillie) Starkey, a twenty-two-year-old woman who had moved to Omaha with her mother.[10] On December 23, 1883, Ferdinand and Tillie married and moved into the St. Charles Hotel.[11] In early 1884, the newly married Ferdinand struck out on his own and formed a partnership with Oliver C. Campbell called Campbell and Joslin. They would manage the Arcade Hotel and Restaurant, located at 1215 Douglas. Their partnership lasted less than a year. By 1885, Oliver Campbell managed the Arcade Hotel alone, and Ferd was again working for his cousin, managing the St. Charles Hotel.[12]

Ferdinand stayed in Omaha for the rest of his life, until his death in 1920. In 1991, George and Sarah Joslyn's twin granddaughters (Joslyn Magowan Birdzell and Sally Magowan Hersey) were interviewed at the Joslyn Art Museum.[13] In their interview, the granddaughters implied that Ferdinand and George were estranged for a period before George's death. According to the twins, Ferd and George had disagreed over George's decision to leave the hotel business and to buy the WNU. This does not appear to have been the case. During Ferd's lifetime, George provided him with a series of positions of ever-decreasing responsibility with his various companies. George provided Ferdinand with jobs as a manager and later as a clerk at his hotels. Later, Ferd would be a stockkeeper, a pressman, and a clerk at the WNU. He worked for his cousin's firm for eleven years, from 1889 until 1900. In 1900, Ferdinand began a part-time career as an apiarist, or beekeeper, on his farm, located at 2510 South Forty-First Street. He continued to drift in and out of jobs with several Omaha companies. Ferdinand never stayed with any of these jobs for long. He ended up working as a night watchman and a common laborer before he retired.[14]

It is not clear what happened to Ferdinand's first wife, Tillie. She may have died, or they may have divorced. She disappeared from the record sometime after 1900. In 1907, Ferdinand returned to Waitsfield for a visit. While there, he married fifty-year-old Mary Wallis Gleason, who lived in nearby Warren, Vermont.[15] After their marriage, the couple returned to Omaha and lived on Ferdinand's farm. Mary remained in Omaha until her death in 1944. Ferdinand and Mary are buried together at Omaha's Forest Lawn Cemetery.[16]

The second family member who arrived in Omaha during this period was George's younger brother, Frederick Abner Joslin. Fred was born in Waitsfield on February 7, 1858. Frederick's life paralleled that of Ferdinand. He lived at home with his father and mother until he married Ina Dana (or perhaps Emma Dana) of Fayston, Vermont in 1883.[17] Two years later, they moved to Omaha, but he did not stay in Omaha as long as Ferdinand did. He also held a variety of jobs for George. Frederick began as a clerk at the St. Charles Hotel. He then managed the hotel for one year, until George quit the hotel business. In 1888, when George bought the Cook Remedy Company, he installed Fred as its first manager. By 1891, Frederick had started his own company. He operated the Marvelous Magic Remedy Company from his residence at 2012 Harney Street. In 1893, Frederick returned to Vermont, where he would remain for the rest of his life.[18] George and his brother appeared to have had a more contentious relationship than George enjoyed with his cousin. It is possible that the disagreement mentioned by Violet's daughters was between Fred and George and not between Ferdinand and George. Regardless of this, George left both Ferdinand and Frederick $5,000 and five hundred shares of stock in his company when he died in 1916.[19]

Another family member who came to Omaha during this era was George's younger sister, Jennie A. Joslin. Jennie was the only daughter of Alfred and Ester Ann Joslin. She was born in Waitsfield on January 12, 1862.[20] She lived with her parents until her mid-teens, when she went to live with Wilber and Alice Joslin. In the 1880 census, Jennie listed her relationship with them as that of a cousin. The family employed her as a domestic servant until she married Herbert D. Jones on September 21, 1881. Herbert, who was working as a laborer, lived with Dr. Emory Hooker and his wife, nearby neighbors of Wilber and Alice.[21] In 1885, Jennie and Herbert moved to Omaha, and Herbert began working as a clerk at the Metropolitan.

It is not clear how long Jennie remained married to Herbert or what happened to him. The *1886 Omaha City Directory* listed H. D. Jones as a clerk at the Windsor Hotel in Omaha. The 1887 directory did not list an H. D. Jones. In 1888, Jennie was listed as Mrs. Jennie Jones, living at 116 South Tenth Street. It is possible that Herbert came to Omaha to work for George and then left both his job and his wife in 1887. It is also possible that he had died. However, Jennie was not listed as a widow in the city directory, a common practice at the time.

In 1889, Jennie moved in with her brother Frederick at 2014 Harney Street. She began working for Nathaniel Falconer at NB Falconer, a dry-goods store located at 1501–1507 Douglas Street.[22] While working there, she met William M. Spence, who worked as a salesman for Falconer. After a brief courtship, Jennie and William were married on May 16, 1889.[23] On April 15, 1890, Jennie gave birth to their daughter, Jessie. William died in November 1908, leaving Jennie and her daughter to live alone at 1309 S. Thirty-First Street.[24] In 1910, Jessie married John Brain, who operated the Omaha School Supply Company with his brother Edwin.[25] John and Jessie moved into a home located at 5114 Burt Street in 1914. In 1915, Jennie moved into the house next door at 5116 Burt.[26] Jennie later married Frank McHenry.[27] She died in Omaha in December 1936.[28]

The final relative to enter the picture during this period was Angie Boyce. Angie was the daughter of Eugene H. Boyce and Lucelia (Lucy) Sophia Selleck, Sarah's older sister. Lucelia was born in Fayston, Vermont, on December 28, 1837.[29] Eugene Boyce grew up as a neighbor of the Sellecks. The son of Don and Clara Boyce, he was born on August 8, 1843.[30] When Eugene was twenty-two, he married the twenty-eight-year-old Lucelia. Their daughter, Angie, was born in 1869.[31] Lucelia died on October 28, 1878, leaving behind her husband and nine-year-old daughter.[32]

Some individuals interviewed about the family believed that the Joslyns raised Angie after Lucy died. The available evidence about Angie's whereabouts during her childhood is sketchy. The 1881 Canadian census listed her as living with her father. In 1881, Eugene Boyce lived in a suburb of Montreal and worked as a machine operator. In addition to his twelve-year-old daughter, Angie, his household included his new wife, twenty-three-year-old Jane Aspinal, a native of Quebec.[33] Seven years later, Miss Angie Boyce was first mentioned in the *1888 Omaha City Directory*, living with the Joslyns at 2522 Davenport. After 1888, she remained with George and Sarah until she married Coit L. Farnsworth in 1892.[34]

What happened to her between 1881 and 1888 is not clear. It was uncommon to list minor children or spouses in city directories. Children would normally receive their own listing when they turned sixteen. Since Angie's first listing was when she was nineteen, we can assume she remained with her father and stepmother in Canada. However, she may have visited the Joslyns frequently before 1887, perhaps staying with them for extended periods.

Regardless of when Angie came to Omaha, George and Sarah were apparently quite fond of their niece. She lived with them until she was twenty-three years old, moving with them to their new home at 2111 Emmett Street. She accompanied them on extended trips, including one in February 1888, which ended with a stay in Montreal to visit her father and to enjoy the winter carnival.[35] She was recognized in George's will and given the same inheritance as Ferdinand and Frederick ($5,000 and five hundred shares of stock in the WNU).[36]

After she married Coit, the couple became very close to George and Sarah. George took a great interest in the couple's welfare. He arranged for Coit to manage the Cook Remedy Company after it had relocated to Chicago. In 1910, George made Coit treasurer of the Western Newspaper Union. Coit was later involved with George's Western Paper Company and the Western Chemical Company.

Even after the couple married, the Joslyns continued to take Angie on extended trips with them. Shortly after George's death, Sarah asked Coit and Angie to accompany her to California. The couple remained with her for two months.[37] Angie served on the boards of several charities that Sarah was involved with, and Sarah later placed Coit on the board of directors of her museum. Coit was also the original coexecutor of Sarah's estate, but he died in 1937, before Sarah's death.[38] It is not surprising that the Joslyns took such an interest in Angie. Their only son had died in infancy, and they had no other immediate family. By surrounding themselves with Ferdinand, Frederick, Jennie, and Angie, they had some semblance of a family.

During this period, George and Sarah met several other individuals who would play important roles in their lives. The first person was John McDonald. McDonald was born in 1861 on Prince Edward Island in Canada.[39] He reportedly met George and Sarah in 1885 when he stopped at the Metropolitan Hotel while on a trip to California. McDonald maintained a close relationship with the family until Sarah's death.

McDonald had studied at McGill University in Montreal. It may have been his familiarity with Montreal that first interested the Joslyns. After meeting them, McDonald decided to stay in Omaha. He later summoned his classmate David Ogilevy and his younger brother, James, to join him there. By 1886, McDonald had established an office in Omaha and was living at 907 South Twentieth Street. In 1887, Ogilevy arrived in Omaha, and they formed the partnership of McDonald & Ogilevy. They remained partners until 1892, when Ogilevy left the partnership. In 1889, McDonald's younger brother James arrived in Omaha and began working for the partnership as a draftsman. James stayed with the company until 1893.[40]

George and Sarah took an interest in McDonald's career and were influential in helping him gain many architectural commissions. The Joslyns gave him several commissions themselves, allowing McDonald to design every structure they built. In 1897, George asked McDonald to design Lynhurst's outbuildings and castle.[41] Perhaps the most important structure he was involved with in Omaha was the Joslyn Memorial Art Museum. In 1922, Sarah hired McDonald and his son, Alan, who had joined his father's architectural business in 1916, to design the structure and manage the project.

Another individual in Omaha during the Joslyns' hotel years was Oliver Carlisle Campbell. Oliver was Ferdinand's partner in the Arcade Hotel, and he seemed to have a close relationship with George. In newspaper accounts of George's funeral, Oliver was listed as an honorary pallbearer.[42] Being an honorary pallbearer is considered an honor normally reserved for close friends, family, or important business associates. Oliver was born in Waitsfield on June 5, 1833.[43] Given the town's small size, it is very likely that George knew Oliver's family.

Oliver and his wife, Charlotte, arrived in Omaha in 1870. The *1870 Omaha City Directory* listed his occupation as real estate developer. Before the Joslyns' arrival in 1880, Oliver briefly became the city's assistant postmaster. At the time, this was a political appointment, so it may indicate that Oliver had some influence in local politics. After serving as assistant postmaster, Oliver went on to manage a number of important properties in Omaha. After his short-lived partnership with Ferdinand ended in 1885, Oliver remained the proprietor and manager of the Arcade Hotel until 1890. In 1914, he became president of the Forest Lawn Cemetery Association.[44]

By 1892, George and Sarah were well-established in Omaha, and they had made many friends in the city. One Omaha native the couple met was an attorney named William Redick. Redick was the son of wealthy Omaha lawyer John Redick, who had made a substantial fortune in real estate. In 1904, William was appointed a district judge in the Fourth District. Redick and his wife accompanied the Joslyns on several trips, and he remained one of their most trusted friends until his death in 1936. In 1928, he helped Sarah found her Society of Liberal Arts.

They also met Clement and Lula Belle Chase. Clement was the publisher of Omaha's society newspaper, the *Omaha Excelsior*, and Lula Belle was an accomplished amateur painter. She and Sarah seemed to have a particularly close relationship, and they served together on the boards of several charities. They also shared a passion for art and were involved in one of the first attempts to build an art museum in Omaha in 1914.

Perhaps the most important people George and Sarah met during this period were George and Hattie Bidwell. George Bidwell was born in Connecticut in 1846.[45] He had come to Omaha in the early 1890s to take a position with the Fremont, Elkhorn & Missouri Valley Railroad Company. The company was a small regional railway that ran the "Cowboy Line" from small eastern Nebraska and western Iowa cities to Chadron, Nebraska, a small city in the far northwest corner of the state.[46] On June 26, 1896, Bidwell was named the company's general manager.[47] In 1903, the smaller railroad was absorbed into the Chicago & Northwestern Railroad. After the merger, Bidwell became the manager of the railroad's operations in Nebraska and Wyoming.

Like George and Sarah, the Bidwells were also involved in many civic and charitable projects. When planning began for the Trans-Mississippi Exposition in 1897, George Bidwell served on its board of directors. The couples may have met when both were involved with the exposition. It was about this time that the two couples began traveling together. The Bidwells shared the Joslyns' passion for travel, and they took frequent trips together. They traveled in style, often sharing private railroad cars. The small resort community of Hot Springs, South Dakota, with its natural hot springs and gorgeous scenery, was a favored destination. After George and Sarah bought their estate of Camp Bord Du Lac, on the banks of Lake Saratoga, in 1903, the Bidwells became frequent guests, often spending the entire summer with their hosts.

In August 1909, Bidwell retired from the railroad, and he and his wife moved to Hollywood, California.[48] They built a mansion next to one owned by Gurdon Wattles, another Omaha friend. After they moved, the Joslyns and Bidwells settled into an interesting routine. During the spring and summer, the Bidwells would stay with George and Sarah at Lynhurst or at Camp Bord Du Lac. During the winter months the Bidwells would reciprocate, and the Joslyns would travel to Hollywood to stay at the Bidwell mansion called Want-A-Teepee.[49]

Want-A-Teepee was a large, white stucco mansion with orange trim, perched high above the fledgling city of Los Angeles. The choice of the name indicates that Bidwell had a well-developed sense of irony. Palm trees and lush gardens surrounded the house. The view from the front veranda was stunning. On a clear day, it was possible to see the entire Los Angeles basin and the blue waters of the Pacific Ocean. The Bidwells and the Joslyns remained close until shortly after George's death in 1916.

By the beginning of 1893, everything was going very well for the Joslyns. The WNU was thriving, and the couple had become wealthy. They were living in a large house on Emmett Street. Their habit of taking frequent extended trips was well established, and they began to spend their summers in New York at Lake Saratoga.

3

The Grounds of Lynhurst
(1893–1897)

The Beginnings of Lynhurst

Although today referred to as the Joslyn Castle, the Joslyns originally called their estate Lynhurst. The reason they picked this name is not clear. Most people assume that they named it after a Scottish castle that had inspired their mansion. George and Sarah supposedly were impressed with a castle they had seen during a tour of Scotland. They came home and requested McDonald to replicate it in Omaha. However, there is little evidence to indicate that George and Sarah ever made a trip to Scotland before the construction of their home. In addition, there appears to be no castle or area of Scotland known as Lynhurst.

There are two other possible explanations for the name. One is that Lyndhurst was the ancient name of the region in southern England from which George's family emigrated to America in the seventeenth century. The Josselyn (Joslin) family settled in this area of England after leaving France in 1044.[1] A second possible explanation is that the Joslyns may have named it after the home of Helen Gould. Her home, Lyndhurst, was a sixty-seven-acre estate in Tarrytown, New York, overlooking the Hudson River. Helen Gould was the daughter of railroad tycoon Jay Gould. She was a well-respected socialite and philanthropist. Her estate was built in the Gothic Revival style. Noted architect Alexander Jackson Davis designed the estate in 1838 for William Paulding. Davis designed the landscape of the estate in the Picturesque and Gardenesque styles.[2]

Picturesque landscaping is the use of plantings to give a landscape a unified pleasing look, creating the effect of a three-dimensional painting. The grounds are planted with attractive plantings, grouped to complement each other and to achieve an idealized whole. Gardenesque landscaping seeks to emphasize individual plants or plantings. To achieve this effect, landscapers use rare and exotic plant species planted in small groupings. The effect is similar to that of a large, showy floral bouquet. The use of rare imported species of plants and flowers is a hallmark of the style. Common in the latter half of the nineteenth century, these are the styles of landscaping used in the design of the landscape at the Joslyns' estate. George reportedly asked McDonald to look at several mansions in the East before he allowed him to design Lynhurst. If Miss Gould's estate and grounds served as their inspiration, perhaps George chose the name to honor its contribution.

The Sutphen Family

The history of the Joslyn estate began in April 1893, when George bought most of the property for his estate from Clinton De Witt Sutphen. George paid Sutphen $65,000 (some accounts say $15,000) and deeded the Joslyn home at 2111 Emmett Street to him.[3] Sutphen took possession of the Joslyn home on May 1, 1893. Shortly after they completed the transaction, George learned that Sutphen did not have a clear title to the property; Sutphen's parents had only willed him a life interest in the property. This meant that while he could use it during his life, he could not sell the property, as it actually belonged to his children.

After discovering this cloud on his title to the land, George initiated a "friendly" lawsuit against Sutphen. Judge Arthur N. Ferguson granted George clear title in 1893.[4] This should have settled the matter, but Sutphen's three children did not agree with the decision, and each of them sought to have it overturned. The problem was in the way Nebraska law was written. The children could appeal the 1893 decision for only one year after reaching the age of majority on their twenty-first birthday.[5]

This led to a series of lawsuits. Sutphen's older son and daughter, Clinton Joy Sutphen and Gladys Kiplinger, brought the first suits. The two siblings sued their father and George Joslyn in 1908.[6] Clinton's suit was dismissed by the district court on February 12, 1910, because he had failed to file it within the one-year statute of limitations. Gladys filed her suit one day before she turned twenty-one. Judge Abraham L. Sutton, who presided over her case, decided this was acceptable. On April 6, 1910, he overturned the 1893 decision and awarded Gladys damages.[7] The third sibling, Earl, also sued when he turned twenty-one. He was one year old in 1893, when the property was sold. His case dragged on until March 22, 1924, when the Nebraska Supreme Court finally decided against him and upheld Judge Ferguson's original 1893 decision.[8] After thirty-one years, the case was finally decided, almost eight years after George had died.

The Columbian Exposition

After purchasing the property, George announced that he and Sarah were moving to Chicago. He added that after settling in Chicago, they would travel to Europe. This may be where the myth originated that a Scottish castle inspired Lynhurst. In reality, there is no evidence that they ever made the European trip.

Even though George had said the couple was relocating to Chicago, it is unlikely that they ever seriously considered a permanent move to Chicago. They were only there for a brief period. It appears the trip to Chicago was related to planning the landscaping and construction of their estate. The best evidence for this theory is several newspaper accounts of the property written in August 1897, describing a charity event that George and Sarah had hosted. The papers reported on the landscaping in detail. The grounds were described as being almost complete, and the articles mention that the new concrete pond and swimming pool were in place. This was three years and four months after the Joslyns had bought the property. George often said that creating the beautiful landscape of his estate was his proudest achievement. Given the extensive amount of effort put into its landscaping, work on the grounds must have started shortly after the Joslyns acquired the property.

This theory is further borne out by their actions during the summer of 1893. After moving out of their home on Emmett Street, George and Sarah lived briefly at the original Paxton Hotel in downtown Omaha. By early June 1893, they were residing at 5804 Rosalie Court in the Hyde Park area of Chicago.[9] In early August, they moved from there to the Hotel Imperial, then located at 1224 Michigan Avenue in Chicago.[10] They remained at the hotel for at least seven weeks before leaving for Saratoga Springs, New York. These addresses are significant and provide clues about what the Joslyns were doing. The significance of the second address is dealt with in Chapter 5. The first address helps solve a mystery about their estate's landscaping. It provides clues as to who designed it and what may have inspired George to put so much effort and money into it.

Rosalie Court was an area of summer homes within three blocks of Jackson Park, on the south side of Chicago. After the area was annexed by the City of Chicago in 1909, the street names were changed, and the street is now called South Harper Avenue.[11] In 1893, the Joslyns lived in this neighborhood for at least a month during the run of the Columbian Exposition. The Exposition, held in Jackson Park from May 1 through October 30, 1893, was one of the largest events of its kind in the nation's history. Admissions to the Exposition numbered 27.5 million, and it was one of the few world's fairs or expositions to come close to actually making a profit.[12]

Newspapers dubbed the Exposition's grounds and buildings the "White City." What made the Exposition so dazzling was not the individual buildings, but the fact that their rooflines were all of a uniform height and that they were all painted the same brilliant white color. Another remarkable feature of the Exposition was the masterful way the grounds and buildings were integrated into one coherent and beautiful entity. This integration of buildings and landscaping into a pleasing, coherent whole is known as the City Beautiful movement. Started as a response to the unsanitary and haphazard conditions then prevalent in most large metropolitan areas, the movement tried to improve urban life through the introduction of parks and coherent urban planning. Many architectural scholars feel the Columbian Exposition grounds and buildings were the first, and perhaps one of the finest, examples of this approach. Many also felt that the masterful landscape design of Frederick Law Olmstead contributed to this strikingly beautiful effect.

Olmstead, the designer of New York City's Central Park, was the foremost landscape architect of his day and a master of Picturesque landscape design. A number of architectural historians consider the grounds of the Exposition one of his firm's finest achievements. Olmstead was also an early proponent of using native species and designing landscapes appropriate to their natural settings. The goal of his approach was to create a pleasing environment that appeared to be an extension of the natural environment.

Another individual who was perhaps equally responsible for the stunning beauty of the exhibition grounds was John Thorpe. On August 22, 1891, the *New York Times* reported that the management of the Exposition had named Thorpe their chief of floriculture. He worked as the assistant to Chief John M. Samuels, who managed the horticultural displays at the Exposition.[13] It was not a match made in heaven. Samuels, a breeder of fruit trees, saw the horticultural displays as a chance to educate the public about American agriculture and to promote agricultural products.

Thorpe was one of the most noted floriculturists in the United States. He was famous for his ability to create stunning and lovely displays of rare flowers and plants. He wanted to dazzle visitors by procuring and displaying the most exotic and beautiful plants he could find. He was able to convince many wealthy families to donate rare species of plants and flowers from their private conservatories to the Exposition.[14]

The management of the Exposition quickly realized that Thorpe's approach appealed to visitors. They gave him carte blanche to control the floral and ornamental plant displays. In the end, he was responsible for all nonagricultural plant displays inside the Horticultural Building. He also controlled the planting of all the flower beds and pots on the Exposition's grounds. He delighted in his work, and he was soon using vast amounts of exhibition space in the Horticultural Building. He was also spending over half the horticultural budget on his projects. When Chief Samuels complained to the Exposition's management about this, the managers sided with Thorpe. Finally, after Samuels vowed not to approve any more of Thorpe's expenditures, the managers quietly told Thorpe to bypass Samuels and send his invoices directly to them.[15]

It is not surprising that the two men refused to speak to one another by the end of the Exposition, or that Thorpe resigned his post in disgust the day the Exposition ended.[16] The management's decision to back Thorpe seems sound in hindsight. While Olmstead's beautiful and natural landscape may have soothed visitors, Thorpe's breathtaking flower beds and planters with exotic plants and flowers around every corner delighted and amazed them. Thorpe's contributions were what many remembered most about their time in the White City.

The Landscape Architects

One enduring mystery about the Joslyn estate was who designed its landscape. Contemporary theory held that Jens Jensen, an exceptionally talented landscape architect from Chicago, had designed the grounds. Jensen did do design work for the Joslyn Castle after it was damaged in 1913, but there is no record of his working on the original design of the estate's landscape.

A second problem with attributing the design to Jensen is that Lynhurst's grounds were not designed in his style. He was an early proponent of the Prairie School of landscape architecture. He felt strongly that landscapers should use native species in plantings and that landscaped grounds should exist in harmony with their environment, instead of being imposed on it. Finally, Jensen did not have a private practice at the time Lynhurst's grounds were designed. He worked for the City of Chicago's Park Department from 1893 to 1897.[17]

There are other, better candidates for the design. Several noted architects designed their landscapes in the Picturesque and Gardenesque styles. One likely candidate was Rudolf Ulrich. He had also been involved with the Columbian Exposition. He favored the Picturesque style, and the timeline for the work at Lynhurst matched. (After his work at the Columbian Exposition, Ulrich came to Omaha in 1897 to serve as the head landscape architect at the Trans-Mississippi Exposition, held in Omaha in 1898.) While it was far from clear who designed the landscape of the Joslyns' estate, period photographs taken of the grounds reveal that their design was the work of a master architect.

A recently discovered article, originally published in the August 29, 1897 edition of the *Omaha World-Herald*, finally solved the mystery. It identified John Thorpe as one of the two designers of the estate's grounds.[18] This explains a great deal. Thorpe reveled in the use of exotic species to create his plantings. By definition, he was a proponent of the Gardenesque movement, using idealized groupings of exotic plants set apart from their natural environment. His approach is much more consistent with the grounds of Lynhurst, where the Joslyns imported rare mature trees and plants from all over the world to create a spectacular landscape.

The Joslyns had lived within walking distance of the Exposition's east gates. Their arrival coincided with the dedication of the Nebraska building on June 8, 1893, an event attended by over two thousand Nebraskans. Since Sarah had assisted in fund-raising efforts for the building's flag and stained-glass window, it is likely they attended this event.[19] After the dedication, they spent a month at Rosalie Court. They spent much of this time attending the Exposition.[20] They would have enjoyed Thorpe's creations every day—the beautiful specimens of exotic flowers, plants, and trees from all over the world at the horticultural exhibit and on the Exposition's grounds. They may have even met Thorpe during this visit.

The other known designer of the castle's landscape was Charles G. Carpenter. According to the *Omaha City Directory*, Carpenter first appeared in Omaha in 1887. He worked as a transit man, or surveyor, for the City of Omaha. He continued his career with the city and became a field engineer in 1889. He left his job in 1895 to begin his own landscaping firm, which was located near the Joslyn estate. During his years at the city, he had probably worked with the noted landscape designer H. W. S. Cleveland. In 1889, the Omaha Parks Commission hired Cleveland to design the city's parks and boulevard system. He designed the Elmwood, Miller, and Fontenelle parks. He also produced the initial design of Riverview Park, now the site of Omaha's Henry Doorly Zoo. Besides the parks, Cleveland designed a series of broad, tree-lined boulevards connecting the parks. Although many Omaha residents met his plans with lukewarm enthusiasm, the system was installed according to his design and still exists in much the same form today. After his death, Omahans warmed to his design, and recently the City of Omaha named a new boulevard in his honor.

Working with Cleveland probably persuaded Carpenter to leave his job and open his own company to meet the growing demand for professional landscaping. Carpenter's private practice fits the timeline for the estate's landscaping perfectly, and his name appears on two building permits issued for structures on the estate's grounds. The first, for the greenhouse, was issued on August 18, 1897. The second, for the brick gate and the gardener's house, was issued on September 30, 1897.[21] By the time these permits were issued, press accounts indicate the landscaping was well underway and that the ponds had been finished. It is difficult to be sure exactly what Thorpe and Carpenter contributed to the design of the estate's landscape. It is safe to assume that both men made significant contributions to the final design. What is clear is that the estate's landscaping must have been stunning, with rare and exotic plants from all over the world.

The Grounds of Lynhurst

The Joslyns hosted a charity event in their yard on Tuesday, August 24, 1897, to benefit the Visiting Nurse Association. Local reporters covered it extensively, and their articles provide a wealth of information about the estate's grounds. Most of the reporters seemed to be quite impressed with what they saw. The *Omaha Excelsior* reporter described the aquatic plantings in the pond and the electric lighting surrounding the ponds as "presenting a fairy-like spectacle."[22]

The *Omaha World-Herald* columnist who covered the occasion also commented on the lush, exotic nature of the grounds. He mentioned that the Joslyns had already planted over one hundred fruit trees on the north side of the property, and that an additional 125 specimen trees and seven hundred shrubs would be planted in the spring. He also noted that an ingenious system of underground pipes constantly watered the trees. Unfortunately, the types of trees and shrubs that the Joslyns planned to plant in the spring were not mentioned.[23]

The most detailed record of the landscape was a study conducted after Sarah's death. In 1944, the Omaha Public School System took control of the property. It asked Frank Pipal, the Omaha city forester, to survey the plants on the grounds. His enthusiastic report listed forty-eight varieties of trees, thirty types of shrubs, and ten varieties of vines that were still growing on the property. He pointed out that the ginkgo, smoke tree, golden rain tree, ironwood, red oak, and English oak were rare in Nebraska and that the trees were beautiful specimens. Of the six trees highlighted by Pipal, some still survive on the castle grounds.[24]

The tree that most excited Pipal was the ginkgo tree. This tree still exists on the property and is located southwest of the front entrance of the castle, on the south side of the front drive. It is approximately fifty feet tall. Fan-shaped leaves divided into two lobes easily identify the tree. The seeds of the ginkgo form in the spring in small clusters, approximately one inch in diameter, and are usually a bright yellow. Ginkgo trees were rare in the United States when George had the Lynhurst specimen planted. The trees, which are quite hardy and prized for their lovely canopies, are used extensively in ornamental gardens. The history of the ginkgo tree dates back 270 million years. The trees have life spans of over a thousand years. The oldest known tree, located in China, is 3,500 years old.[25]

Besides the exotic trees and plants, the Lynhurst landscape featured stone planters, trellises, birdhouses, and formal garden beds. The planters and a birdbath were fashioned into a variety of whimsical shapes from tufa limestone. (Tufa is a highly porous form of limestone that resembles lava.) Remnants of these planters and the birdbath are still visible in the yard in front of the castle. The original raised circular concrete planting bed still exists directly in front of the house, surrounded by the front walk. Sarah used to have flowers planted in this bed in a large, formal star-shaped pattern. The eastern lawn showcased a twenty-foot-long, six-foot-high cast-iron pergola, molded to resemble large, rough-hewn log beams and covered with ivies and grapevines. Sarah had young men at a local reformatory build several large and ornate wooden birdhouses for her, and these dotted the grounds of the estate. In the evening, lanterns (and later, electric lights) placed on poles illuminated the grounds.

The highlights of the landscaping were two adjoining concrete pools to the west of the house. The gardeners planted the northern pond with water lilies and other aquatic plants. The larger southern pool was used for swimming. A small concrete bridge spanned the two pools. It concealed a barrier that kept the water in the pools from mixing. Exotic plantings surrounded both pools. Nearby there was a discreetly camouflaged entrance into an underground changing grotto. During the summer, the Joslyns hosted swimming parties, and the pools were quite popular with neighborhood children.

Today, little remains of the original landscape. Most of the rare trees have died, and several other changes have been made to the estate. In 1949, the Omaha Public School System (OPS) tore down the gardener's house after vandals had severely damaged it. The large wrought-iron gates were removed from the entrances and placed in storage. OPS added a large parking lot on the eastern side of the property. The school system filled in the ponds for insurance reasons and removed the concrete bridge railings. The base of the bridge is still visible directly west of the castle. OPS removed the plantings that surrounded the pools, and the area was covered with sod to lower maintenance costs. Part of the wrought-iron fence was donated by OPS to World War II scrap-metal drives. In several areas, the limestone walls are crumbling from water damage.

Even with all these changes, the attentive visitor can still see glimpses of what once existed. The wrought-iron gates for the walking paths remain, each with George's initials in their centers. The front walk leading to the castle's entrance still exists, as does the concrete flower bed. The landscape still has its pleasing, undulating contours. Walking around the perimeter of the grounds and viewing the Joslyn Castle from different angles is one of the best ways to appreciate what the grounds once must have looked like. The way the contour of the grounds complements the castle and other buildings is readily apparent and is a tribute to the designers. With a small effort, one can still envision the grounds as they looked in their prime and be both saddened at their loss and stirred by their remaining beauty.

The Visiting Nurses' Charity Event

By the time the visiting nurses' event was held, officials from around the United States and from several foreign countries had arrived to supervise the construction of their buildings and pavilions at the Trans-Mississippi Exposition, an event planned for the following summer. One of these officials, Mr. Ebell, the commissioner of the Russian trade delegation, wanted to express his goodwill toward his host city and became involved with the Joslyn event. He had a small replica of a Russian tearoom constructed at the Joslyns' estate. It offered guests an opportunity to sample authentic Russian tea. His wife, Camille, managed the tearoom. His involvement, and the presence of the other foreign visitors in Omaha, inspired the organizers of the event to adopt an international theme that would mimic the coming exposition. This gave the evening a decidedly cosmopolitan flair.[26]

This occasion is also important because it was quite possibly the largest event ever held at Lynhurst. While no attendance figures are available, an analysis of the admission receipts indicates that over two thousand people attended the event.[27] A major draw was the opportunity to see the grounds and pools firsthand.

Descriptions of the event note that the event's organizers strung white sailcloth completely around the perimeter of the property, deterring curious onlookers from getting a free look. In addition to Mr. Ebell's tearoom, there was a Gypsy tent with fortunetellers; a dairy maids' booth, where milk and cheese sandwiches were available; a Japanese tea garden; a refreshment booth; and a candy booth. An electrically illuminated pyramid of flowers stood on the east end of the lawn. The entire grounds was illuminated by small, multicolored electric lights strung on the trees and trellises. The Joslyns had arranged for male visitors to be able to rent swimsuits and use the swimming pool. The Twenty-Second Infantry Band from nearby Fort Crook, led by Colonel Wycoff, provided the music for the event. During the evening, several prominent young men sang popular songs for the crowd, accompanied by the band.[28]

The highlight of the evening came when George brought out two of his thoroughbred horses to perform for the crowd. George and Sarah owned four famous thoroughbreds. They took great pride in the animals, and they showed them at least once at the annual New York City horse show at Madison Square Garden in 1894. Sarah's horse, Bay Chief, placed second in class, and George's horse, Maney Bond, won honorable mention.[29] The horses were extremely intelligent, and George had once hired a circus trainer to train them to do a variety of tricks. Among other talents, the horses could bow, retrieve dropped handkerchiefs, count with their hooves, and dance.[30] George enjoyed showing off his horses throughout his life.

4

Building the Castle of Lynhurst
(1898–1903)

Orchid Mania

Shortly after the benefit for the visiting nurses, Sarah set off for New York City on a monthlong trip to purchase plants for the Joslyns' recently completed conservatory. Their first conservatory was a brick, metal, and glass building measuring thirty-six by forty feet, with 1,440 square feet of floor space. It was erected over several months and finished in September 1897.[1] George and Sarah had the structure built to house a collection of orchids they had begun. They would continue to collect orchids and other rare tropical plants until 1913. As their collection grew, they expanded their conservatory and constructed a large greenhouse on their estate. They later added two extensions to the conservatory, expanding it to 2,080 square feet. The greenhouse was built in four sections; it measured twenty-two by one hundred feet and added 2,200 square feet of space.[2] George and Sarah later connected the conservatory and greenhouse with a glass-enclosed potting area that measured forty by forty-eight feet, bringing the total greenhouse and conservatory space to 6,200 square feet. In 1903, they added the final conservatory attached to their mansion, expanding the total space to 6,532 square feet.[3] This small conservatory is the last vestige of the once-enormous conservatory-greenhouse complex.

Orchid collecting was quite popular at the end of the nineteenth century, especially in England. Several wealthy individuals in England and the United States created very large and expensive collections. Some people became such avid collectors that they were said to suffer from "orchid mania" or "orchid delirium." As orchid collections grew in size and expense, there was a very real competition among wealthy collectors to have the largest and most impressive collection.

Although orchids had been imported to England and Europe since before 1800, orchid mania began around 1850 after the popularization of "Wardian" cases invented by English physician Dr.

Nathaniel Bagshaw Ward. Ward's cases were constructed of a metal or wooden frame with glass panels set on all sides and were basically forerunners of the modern terrarium.[4] Orchids and other rare tropical plants had a much better chance of arriving in England or America in good condition in these cases. Prior to the adoption of these glass shipping cases, it was common for whole shipments consisting of thousands of rare plants to arrive at their destination with every plant dead. The adoption of the Wardian case fueled the passion for collecting orchids and significantly increased the size and diversity of large collections. There were several noted collectors in America when the Joslyns began their collection. One, Erastus Corning, had built an orchid collection containing an estimated 7,500 individual plants by the time of his death in 1897.[5] His collection was surpassed by that of Helen Gould, who grew 8,000 orchids in one section of the large greenhouse at her estate, Lyndhurst.[6] By 1902, Mrs. George B. Wilson of Philadelphia, the wife of a wealthy real estate developer, had amassed a collection of over 15,000 orchids, housed in eleven large greenhouses and valued at $300,000. Mrs. Wilson had created her collection in less than ten years, primarily by buying the entire collections of other large collectors, such as that of Mr. Corning.[7]

Along with the increasing size of the collections came a demand for rarer orchids. A serious collector would want to have the only specimen of a rare orchid as the centerpiece of his or her collection. This demand for rare plants drove the record prices for orchids ever higher. In 1906, a single orchid was auctioned off in London for $6,000.[8] To fill the increased demand for orchids and other rare plants, several orchid dealers employed the services of orchid hunters, who would scour the globe in search of the rarest and most beautiful specimens.

The orchid industry was bitterly competitive. Two of the largest and most dominant firms were located in England. The first was Veitch & Sons of Exeter and the second was the F. Sander Company of St. Albans.[9] Each firm employed the services of over twenty full-time orchid hunters to search for new orchids and other rare plants. In addition to the commercial hunters, private hunters worked for wealthy patrons and for expeditions sponsored by universities and scientific institutions.

It was a perilous occupation. Mrs. Wilson's orchid hunter, Harry Barrault, lost two of his assistants to malaria during a hunt in the jungles of Colombia in 1901.[10] Sander & Company lost at least five of its most experienced hunters to a variety of causes.[11] Orchid hunters were incredibly brave and desperate men who took huge risks to obtain their prizes.

Orchid hunters showed little regard for the environment, finding that the most expedient way to collect orchids was to cut down the trees on which the orchids grew. The average number of orchids collected from each tree in this manner was three, and these hunters were shipping well over a hundred thousand orchids a year back to Europe and America.[12] The intensely competitive hunters would often set an area on fire after they had finished collecting its orchids. If rival hunters happened on one another during their collection trips, they would often attempt to hijack or destroy the orchids their competitor had collected; however, most of them stopped short of actually attempting to kill their rivals.[13]

Whether George and Sarah knew of the more unsavory aspects of their new obsession is unknown. Throughout their lives, the Joslyns seem to adopt the hobbies of those individuals at the upper reaches of wealth and society. They owned and showed thoroughbred horses and dogs, and their animals often won prizes in their classes. Orchid collecting fits into this pattern. In the 1890s, orchids were expensive and difficult to care for. Only very wealthy individuals had the resources needed to amass large collections. Perhaps adopting the hobbies of the ultrarich was the Joslyns' way of stating that they too had arrived at the upper echelons of society.

Regardless of their motivation, George and Sarah quickly became serious orchid collectors. In 1913, when they ceased collecting, their collection contained over 1,200 individual orchids representing more than a thousand species.[14] The Joslyn orchid collection was one of the finest in the Midwestern United States. The Joslyns collected orchids from all over the world, and only George, Sarah, and their head gardener, Isaac Roman, were allowed to tend them. In addition to their orchids, the Joslyns reportedly had the finest collection of crotons west of Chicago, and the centerpiece of their palm house was a huge bougainvillea vine that grew to the top of the palm house's thirty-foot-high dome.[15]

A later press account reported that Sarah had traveled throughout Asia and Europe in search of rare specimens and had personally collected many of the rarest orchids.[16] While she had several opportunities to travel to Europe, it is very unlikely she ever traveled to Asia. Most of the largest orchid dealers were located in England and Belgium, and they already had hunters searching the globe for orchids. The travel time to Europe was also much shorter; at the time, Sarah could have left Omaha and docked in a European port in about ten days. A trip to Europe might have lasted as little as one or two months.

The only plant-buying trip the couple ever made that was recorded in detail was the 1897 trip mentioned eariler.[17] Several large American orchid dealers were headquartered in New York, including the firm of Siebrecht & Wadley, which was located on Fifth Avenue.[18] It would have been very easy for George and Sarah to build their collection without ever leaving the United States. Sarah may also have employed a private orchid hunter to gather specimens for her collection; or perhaps, like Mrs. Wilson, she built her collection by attending the frequent auctions of collections that occurred after the deaths of other orchid fanciers. However George and Sarah acquired their collection, there is little doubt that they took it seriously and were very proud of it.

Sarah and the Trans-Mississippi Exposition

After the fall of 1897, efforts to complete the landscaping of the property continued, but little work was done on the structures planned for the property. Beyond plantings in the conservatory and small projects, major work on the estate's buildings did not resume until the summer of 1900. The building permit for the carriage house, the next major structure on the estate, was not issued until July 9, 1900.[19] Two events that occurred during this period may explain these delays. The first was the

Trans-Mississippi Exposition, which was held in Omaha between June 1 and October 31, 1898. The second was the arrival of the Joslyns' young ward, Violet Carl, sometime around 1897.

By the time of the visiting nurses event at the Joslyns' estate, the construction of the Trans-Mississippi Exposition buildings and grounds was well underway. Construction on such a massive scale must have strained the resources of the city and put many smaller construction projects on hold. This drain on contractors and builders probably lasted until shortly after the gates of the Exposition opened on May 1, 1898.

As planning for the Trans-Mississippi Exposition continued, Sarah became a board member of the Exposition's Ladies' Bureau of Entertainment, a committee of forty prominent Omaha women. They determined what to exhibit at the Mines and Mining building that would be of interest to women and children. Sarah served on the board of the committee with nine other women. They had offices and a salon on the second floor of the Mines building. They took their work seriously, and in the end were responsible for one-fourth of the exhibit space in the building.[20]

One of their proudest achievements was organizing the flower parade held on Friday, August 5, 1898. The parade consisted of forty carriages decorated with a variety of paper flowers. Sarah and her friend, Lula Belle Chase, rode in the third carriage, which was decorated with white and red paper poppies. Sarah wore a white ankle-length gown with a matching large-brimmed hat and parasol. Mrs. Chase was also dressed in a white outfit, and wore a Gainsborough hat. After the parade, the organizers awarded silver medallions to the three most beautifully decorated carriages. Unfortunately, Sarah and her friend did not win one of them. They later received medallions after the organizing committee decided that all of the parade's participants deserved recognition.[21]

After their parade, the Ladies' Bureau helped plan the festivities held during the visit of President William McKinley in October 1898. The president's train arrived on the evening of Tuesday, October 11, at about 8:00 PM. Exposition officials and other dignitaries met President McKinley. They escorted the president in a procession of thirty-six carriages to Omaha's City Hall and then to a dinner held in his honor at the Omaha Club. Sarah, Mrs. J. E. Summers Jr., Mrs. Howland, and Miss Humphrey rode in the thirty-first carriage in the procession.[22] At the dinner, Sarah was seated at a table with the Chinese and Korean ministers traveling with the presidential party, Minister Wu Ting Fang and Minister Chin Pom Ye respectively. The next day, she was among the group that accompanied the president to the Exposition. That evening, she and George attended a final dinner for the president at the Omaha Club before he left for St. Louis the next morning. This appears to be the first time that either George or Sarah met a serving U.S. president.[23]

For many years, the Joslyn Memorial Museum had a display on its lower level commemorating the Trans-Mississippi Exposition. This may have been a reflection of how much the exposition meant to Sarah, and she might have requested that the museum install the display. Alternatively, it may have been a museum curator's attempt to highlight an important event in the life of the museum's founder. One can assume that their experiences in 1898, just eighteen years after arriving in Omaha and living over a printing shop, must have affected George and Sarah. In less than twenty years, the couple had acquired control of a large company and amassed a personal fortune. They were building the largest mansion in Omaha and were considered pillars of their community.

Violet Carl

The other major event that occurred during the lull in construction was the arrival of Violet Carl. Violet's origins are hazy, as is the story of how she came to live with the Joslyns. All that seems to be known for certain about her is that she was born on August 7, 1892.[24] She probably came to live with George and Sarah when she was five or six years old.

In their 1991 interview, Violet's twin daughters, Joslyn and Sally, reported that their mother had told them several times that she was five when she moved into the Joslyn household. They explained that their mother had told them that their great-grandmother had cared for Violet until she was five. When she could no longer take care of the little girl, she sent Violet to live with the Joslyns. Finally, the twins said that George and Sarah had intended to adopt their mother, but the adoption proceedings were not handled correctly, and she was never formally adopted. There is little in the historic record that supports or refutes their account. No one has ever discovered Violet's birth certificate, and there is no record of her birth in Douglas County records.

There may be more evidence as to the nature of the Joslyns' relationship with the girl. Adoption was a much less formal process when Violet came to live with the Joslyns. (Nebraska did not institute laws regulating adoptions until 1943.)[25] If they wished to adopt Violet, the Joslyns would not have needed a lawyer; they could have merely brought her into their home and treated her as their own child.

The best evidence of their true relationship with Violet was Violet's listing in the 1900 census. It lists her as a boarder, and not as their daughter, and identifies her as Violet Carl. In the same census, the Joslyns responded that they did not know which state Violet's mother and father were born in. This suggests that they did not know her origin or who had taken care of the little girl before they met her. A few years later, when Violet was fifteen and began to be mentioned in press accounts about the family, she was still referred to as Violet Carl. Even at her high school graduation from Brownell Academy in 1910, she was listed as Violet Carl.[26] This may indicate that the Joslyns originally thought of her as a ward and did not intend to adopt her.

However, when Violet was in her late teens, she began to be referred to as Violet Joslyn, and she was often identified as the Joslyns' daughter. By the time of Violet's marriage in 1913, this transformation in her identity was complete, and newspapers always identified her as the Joslyns' daughter. Whatever their original intent, over time the Joslyns appeared to change their minds about Violet, and they treated her as their daughter.

A more interesting question, and one seldom asked, is why George and Sarah felt the need to take in the child at this point in their lives. George was fifty years old and Sarah was in her late forties in

1898. They were wealthy and had many friends. They loved to take extended trips around the United States and Canada. George was busy with his company, and Sarah was actively involved with several charities. They were also both busily working on their estate and gardens. It would seem that caring for a young child could only complicate their lives.

Two facts may explain their desire to have a young child in their home. First, Violet's arrival did not seem to herald much of a change in the Joslyns' lifestyle. In 1899, they took several trips to New York State and Hot Springs, South Dakota, and they toured western Canada for several weeks. With their wealth, they could easily have afforded the nurses and nannies needed to care for their young charge, so the child's demands on their time would have been slight.

A second and perhaps more important reason was that Violet filled the void left by the departure of their niece. After George and Sarah returned to Omaha in 1896, their niece Angie stayed in Chicago. She and her husband remained there until at least 1908. The Joslyns always seemed to need the presence of a young woman in their lives: first George's sister Jennie, later their niece Angie, and finally Violet. Possibly the premature death of their only son Clifton in 1873 created a void that they attempted to fill for the rest of their lives.

The Carriage House

Beginning in 1900, construction of Lynhurst's buildings accelerated. The first major building erected was the carriage house. In early 1901, work on the structure was completed, and George and Sarah decided to throw two large parties in the new structure to commemorate this milestone. These parties were two of the most famous and well-documented events that occurred on the property. The parties spanned two nights in May and were the social events of the spring season, with over two hundred people attending each night.

The first evening, Wednesday, May 1, 1901, was a reception from eight to eleven o'clock with the Joslyns receiving their friends as they entered. The second evening was devoted to a large dance. Several of their friends assisted them with their hosting duties on both evenings. Their guest list included almost all the people prominent in Omaha society, including their friend William Redick and his wife. Also among the guests both evenings were George and Hattie Bidwell.

The parties were big hits, and published reports about them appeared in all the Omaha papers. The *Omaha Excelsior* devoted almost an entire page to the parties. This report is valuable because it described the estate grounds and the beautifully decorated carriage house in detail. The account first described the interior of the carriage house, and it is the most complete historical description of the interior of any building on the Joslyns' property.

> The barn, 50 by 72 feet in size, is built of stone from Silverdale, Kansas. All wood used in the interior finish is quarter-sawed oak, and the fixtures, the hangers for the harness and other appliances, are of metallic bronze, beautifully worked. The main room, or coach room, where the dance was held, is a superb apartment of the right proportions for the use it is to be put and

equally right for a dance, of which the *Excelsior* trusts it will see many more. The floor is of hard maple polished like a mirror, and the walls are lined with enameled brick and hung with pictures of famous coaching scenes and other equine exploits. Over the doors opening into the other rooms are art transoms showing horse pictures etched by the sand blast, the ones to the harness room bearing the pictures of the two well-known riding horses, which do so many pretty tricks at the command of their master. The harness room, complete in every detail, and, like the rest of the building, wonderfully 'up to date' in all its appointments, is also lined with enameled brick. The stalls adjoining luxurious boxes for their highbred occupants are lined with St. Louis pressed brick. On the second floor is a suite of rooms for the coachman, complete in all housekeeping appointments if he happens to be a married man. The whole structure is electrically lighted from lamps conveniently placed in artistic holders. There is a washing room where the harness and carriages can be cleaned with new appliances designed for the purpose. In the basement the heating plant is designed not only for the barn, but to convey heat to the new house when finished as well, and to the greenhouses, and here also is a private light plant to cover the premises in any direction, and a refrigerating plant to be connected with the cooling room of the residence-to-be and to the cooler which will be established there for cut flowers from the conservatories.[27]

There are two items of special interest in this account. One is the mention of the three etched-glass art panels over the transoms of the doorways. These still exist in the carriage house. They were once rumored to be portraits of the Joslyns riding in a carriage on one panel and in a horse-drawn sleigh on another. Close examination of the windows belies this assertion. The individuals depicted on the etched-glass panels have no resemblance to anyone connected with the family. (In truth, the images the panels depict are somewhat fanciful.) The two large panels bear a strong resemblance to Currier & Ives prints, which were very fashionable at the time. However, the two horses pictured on the third panel do resemble horses that belonged to George and Sarah. One horse resembles Sarah's famous horse, Bay Chief, and the other resembles George's horse, Search Light. This could be what the article alluded to when it discussed this panel and may explain how the myth about the two other panels started.

The second interesting item in this report is the mention of the cooling plant located in the basement of the carriage house. This was probably the basis for a later erroneous report that the Joslyns' house had an early air-conditioning system. Willis Carrier did not patent his invention of an air-cooling system until after the carriage house was completed. Instead, the account probably refers to a refrigeration device for the walk-in cooler their house originally had.

The *Excelsior* reporter continued to describe the interior of the carriage house in detail; he made a special note of the elaborate floral displays in the building.

Its finely polished floors and gleaming walls of white tiles, with oaken beams overhead, made a ballroom setting that many palatial homes might envy, and with the unlimited supply of plants and flowers from their own greenhouse, Mr. and Mrs. Joslyn made it a bower of exquisite color and perfume. The windows were latticed with ropes of smilax and in each was a box of growing flowers, tulips, lilies of the valley, pansies, begonias and sweet alyssum, while three huge radiators were almost hidden in Easter lilies, pelargoniums and spirea. The stable buckets, bound and monogrammed in brass, stood in a rack at one end of the room filled with hyacinths and the gorgeous pink bloom of the tall bougainvillea, which also filled one corner of the room, luxuriant banks of palms being used in the other corners and to screen the mandolin orchestra from view. Three huge hanging baskets of ivy geranium and asparagus-sprengerii, with its drooping tendrils, hung from the ceiling, making one feel literally surrounded by flowers. The pictures, all of coaches and coaching days, were surrounded by sprays of brilliant Japan quince or the paler blossoms of cherry; even the snowball was forced into an early appearance in one corner, and a tall vase of Golden Gates held sway near a doorway leading into the harnessing room, where red carnations bubbled over from a watering trough in huge clusters.[28]

The carriage house must have been stunning, and the elaborate decorations certainly seemed to affect the individuals who wrote about it. The *Excelsior* writer pointed out, rather wistfully, that many of the guests were envious of the horses that would be moving into the structure soon after the party. The reporter for the *Omaha World-Herald* stated that the potted plants at the affair numbered in the hundreds.[29] Everyone commented on the exquisite beauty of the grounds, where benches had been placed for the guests to sit and enjoy the warm spring evening. The sky was clear and moonlit on both evenings.

The *Excelsior* correspondent continued by reporting on the food and delicacies available at the party: "Supper was served to all during the evening in the box stalls, whose iron gratings were twined with southern smilax and the feeding troughs were filled with candies in exact imitation of shelled corn. The ices were served in the form of ears of corn, apples, watermelons and peaches, and everywhere were flowers, flowers, flowers."[30]

The Scottish Baronial Castle

The parties were supreme successes for George and Sarah. The *Excelsior* reporter mentioned in his article that construction of the main house would begin in the fall of 1901. This was somewhat optimistic; construction of the main house did not begin until the week of March 10, 1902.[31] On April 21, 1902, George took out a building permit for the structure.[32] It was reported that he estimated the structure would be completed in sixteen months and would cost $60,000.[33]

Joslyn had not counted on trouble with the building-trade unions. A series of strikes and work stoppages dragged out the construction schedule. On June 16, 1902, the Teamsters Union stopped work on the estate, refusing to unload materials transported by nonunion workers. In a newspaper account about the strike, a reporter noted that the estimated cost of the mansion had now risen to $100,000.[34] In April, a citywide strike by the Hod Carriers (workers who transported bricks and mortar at construction sites) disrupted construction again. In May, the Teamsters and Carpenters unions both staged citywide strikes. In the end, it took nineteen months to complete the house, and the final cost rose to $250,000.[35] The Joslyns began moving into the Lynhurst mansion in mid-October 1903. By Christmas, they were ready to celebrate the holiday season in their new home.

It was quite a home. It had thirty-four rooms, with over 19,000 square feet of space, arranged on three floors, with a small fourth-floor turret room. The home also had a large finished lower level. It had its own electrical generating system. It reportedly was equipped with an air-filtration system and a centralized vacuum. Ornately carved paneling of rare and exotic hardwoods filled the house. Elaborate plaster architectural flourishes adorned the ceilings. Hand-painted murals decorated at least three of the main-floor rooms. Two of these murals still exist: the rose panels in the gold room and the restored frieze in the morning room. George and Sarah spent an additional $50,000 on interior furnishings.[36] The house boasted such amenities as its own bowling alley, a fully equipped gymnasium, an attached conservatory, a porte-cochere, and a unique floral-display window. When completed, it was the largest mansion, on the most beautifully landscaped grounds, in Omaha.

Unlike the landscaping, there is no doubt about the architect who designed the Joslyn Castle. George commissioned his friend John McDonald to design the structure and oversee its construction. All the building permits issued for structures on the property list McDonald as the architect. He probably chose the final design of the structures himself. Since there is no evidence of a trip to Scotland, it is likely that the Joslyns allowed McDonald to design the structure as he wished, within broad guidelines. Since McDonald was quite proud of his Scottish ancestry, it is logical to assume he is the one who chose to design the structures at Lynhurst in the Scottish Baronial style.

Scottish Baronial was a style of architecture popular in Scotland in the mid-nineteenth century. It was part of a larger movement known as Picturesque Revival architecture, which was prevalent in several European nations. The Picturesque movement attempted to present an idealized and romantic portrait of a nation's past glories through architecture. It achieved this by reviving historic architectural design elements that were part of a country's most notable structures, and using them in the design of new structures.

This movement reflected the growth of nationalism and national pride in European nations. Many nations in the world at the time had versions of a "manifest destiny." One aspect of this was a glorification of their national past. Architects responded by reviving traditional designs identified with a nation's identity. Tudor, Gothic, High Victorian, Norman, and Scottish Baronial were all styles of the Picturesque Revival movement. These styles shared many common design elements, which can make attributing a design to a single school difficult. In addition, individual architects would often modify the design of a structure to suit their individual needs. Thus, few structures are "pristine" examples of a particular revival school. This is perhaps the most important and significant aspect of the Joslyn Castle—it is quite possibly the only large structure in the United States designed in an almost-pure Scottish Baronial style.

Some of the major exterior features of Scottish Baronial architecture are the use of corbelled drum turrets and chimneys, crenellated parapets, bartizans, and corbie gables. The designs were asymmetrical, with offset entrances. Baronial architecture favored a tall, narrow structure. The preferred construction material was stone, and the style was best suited for large structures. The exterior and interior of the structures were decorated with heraldry symbols.[37]

The term corbelling refers to a structure that spreads out at the top by slightly extending each succeeding race, or layer of bricks or stones. This characteristic is most evident on the southeast turret of the castle. A drum turret is simply a turret that is rounded and not angular in shape. Crenellation refers to the upside-down toothlike structures located at the tops of the turrets and over the front entrance of the castle. A bartizan is a small, turret-shaped structure that is an outgrowth on the corners of the upper walls. A mock bartizan decorates the south face of the castle. A gable is the triangular structure at the end of a roof peak. A corbie, or crow-stepped, gable refers to one that is shaped like stair steps.[38] There is an excellent example of a corbie gable on the castle's west side, beside the music room.

In short, revival architects designed homes that resembled medieval castles, with features once vital to a structure's defense reduced to mere ornamentation. The carriage house actually offers a more coherent and purer expression of the Scottish Baronial style. The various elements described above are more pronounced and easier to see on the smaller structure.

McDonald used limestone from Silverdale, Kansas for the exterior walls of all the structures at Lynhurst and for the wall that surrounds the property.[39] Limestone was readily available and could be easily carved into blocks and exterior decorations. Its main drawback is that it is a sedimentary form of stone. The porous nature of this type of stone makes it susceptible to damage from water and airborne pollutants, which are quickly absorbed into the stone. The effect of pollution on the exterior walls of the castle is most visible from the fourth-floor turret room. The small windows in the room provide an opportunity to closely examine the damage that pollutants have done to the exterior. A black residue on the stonework mars the upper wall blocks, and the finial (a small architectural flourish atop the peak of a gable) has an almost melted appearance. Although it may now seem that limestone was a poor choice for the castle's exterior walls, it is important to note that at the time of the castle's construction, urban pollution was not as great a problem as it is today.

GEORGE A. JOSLYN,
PRES. WESTERN NEWSPAPER UNION, PRES. WESTERN
PAPER CO.,
OMAHA.

George as he appeared in 1904 when he was fifty-six years old. This photograph appeared in *Nebraskans 1854–1904*, published by the Omaha Bee Company.

Sarah Joslyn was in her late forties when she served on the entertainment committee of the Trans-Mississippi Exposition in 1898. Contrary to later stories about her, she is dressed in an expensive and elegant gown. Photograph courtesy of the Omaha Public Library.

This Victoria carriage from the Trans-Mississippi Exposition Flower Parade was decorated in a manner similar to Sarah's carriage. Photograph courtesy of the Omaha Public Library.

George and Sarah riding two of their famous thoroughbred horses; George is atop Search Light and Sarah is on Bay Chief. The photograph was taken near Lake Saratoga at Saratoga Springs, New York, during one of the several visits the couple made to the area in the 1890s. Photograph from the Douglas County Historical Society (Archive Collections).

The etched-glass transom in the carriage house may depict two of the Joslyns' thoroughbred horses. The horses' pose and the setting are remarkably similar to the preceding photograph. Photograph by author.

SAFFORD.

A drawing of Safford, one of George and Sarah's St. Bernard dogs, after the dog placed second in his class in the 1892 Omaha dog show. This drawing appeared on the front page of the October 29, 1892 *Omaha Excelsior*.

This is the earliest known photograph of the grounds of Lynhurst. It shows the grounds decorated for the Visiting Nurses charity event, which took place on August 22, 1897. In the foreground are the ponds and Mr. Ebell's Russian tearoom. On the left is the Sutphen farmhouse, where the Joslyns lived until they completed their mansion in 1903. On the right is the home of Charles and Bertha Offutt. Photograph courtesy of the Friends of Joslyn Castle.

George Alfred Joslyn's initials still grace the gates at the entrances of Lynhurst's walking paths.
Photograph by author.

The front of the carriage house provides an excellent illustration of the asymmetry and exterior design elements of a Scottish Baronial structure. Photograph by author.

This detailed view of Lynhurst Castle's southeast drum turret illustrates a form of corbelling and the use of heraldic symbols on the stone band above the window. Photograph by author.

The crenellated roofline of the porte cochere is a design feature identified with Scottish Baronial architecture. Scottish Baronial structures also frequently incorporated peaked Gothic archways and buttressed walls. Photograph by author.

A corbie gable tops the southwest wall along the music room addition. A prominent mock bartizan, or tourelle, is the outgrowth at the top of the corner of the structure. Photograph by author.

Lynhurst Castle as viewed from the east lawn. Photograph by author.

Noted Omaha photographer Louis Bostwick took this photograph of the Joslyns' castle in 1910.
Photograph from the Bostwick-Frohardt collection of the Durham Western Heritage Museum.

A rare photograph of the gardener's house that was once located on the southeast side of the estate. One of gardener Isaac Roman's seven children stands in the foreground of this image. Photograph courtesy of the Roman family and the Friends of Joslyn Castle.

Part of the Joslyns' greenhouse complex is visible on the left side of this photograph, with the carriage house in the background. Photograph courtesy of Lannie McNichols and the Friends of Joslyn Castle.

This undated image offers a view from the bridge spanning the ponds toward the palm conservatory. The curved path and the use of trees and shrubs to frame a visitor's forward view were hallmarks of the Picturesque school of landscape design. Photograph courtesy of the Friends of Joslyn Castle.

A 1916 view of Lynhurst's grounds from the west is another excellent example of a Picturesque landscape. Photograph from the Bostwick-Frohardt collection of the Durham Western Heritage Museum.

5

The Interior of Lynhurst Castle
(1903–1904)

The Interior of the Castle

As impressive as the exterior is, the castle's interior is truly splendid. At first glance, the interior of the mansion appears to be an eclectic mixture of materials and styles; however, particularly on the main floor, they blend to create a subtly elegant and coherent statement. A discussion of the interior begins with the second stop George and Sarah made during their travels in the summer of 1893. After their visit to the Columbian Exposition, they moved to the Hotel Imperial, located at 1224 Michigan Avenue in Chicago. The hotel was next door to the offices of Spierling & Linden at 1226 Michigan Avenue.[1] (Spierling has been universally misspelled as Sperling or Sperlings by individuals writing about the Joslyns.) Spierling & Linden was a well-respected interior-design firm and was considered a leader in its field. The firm is best remembered today for the work of its subsidiary, Linden Glass. Linden Glass produced art-glass and stained-glass windows for various architects. Press accounts of the time credit Spierling & Linden with the interior design of Joslyn Castle. Recent research has tended to support this. Several of the art-glass windows that decorate the castle are consistent with those attributed to Linden Glass. Since none of the art-glass windows in the castle appear to be signed or bear trademarks, it is difficult to prove who produced them. The Joslyns' proximity to the company, and the obvious quality of the windows, suggest Linden Glass Company's involvement. In addition, if Spierling & Linden controlled the design of the interior, the firm would surely have chosen its own in-house company to create the windows.

It is unclear why George and Sarah chose the firm. John McDonald may have recommended it to them, or they may have learned of it after their arrival in Chicago. The extent to which Spierling controlled the design of the interior is also not clear. Recently, shipping information discovered on the back of one of the mahogany panels in the stair hall identified the source of the paneling as the Edmund's Manufacturing Company of Chicago. The firm was located near the corner of Washington and Robey streets, at 571 South Robey, in what was then the western part of Chicago. The *1903 Chicago City Directory* listed Edmund's as a contractor. The firm manufactured wooden paneling and perhaps furniture. That a Chicago firm manufactured the paneling may also indicate that Spierling managed the design of the interior; however, it is also possible that McDonald choose Edmund's because no Omaha firm had the needed expertise.

McDonald's original drawings for the interior rooms indicate that he intended to use Spanish mahogany paneling in all of the first-floor rooms. Instead, each of the six original first-floor rooms is paneled in a different type of exotic hardwood. McDonald may have abandoned his original plans in an effort to make the structure's interior more interesting, or perhaps Spierling & Linden's designers refined his original plans. Since the company was credited with the interior's design, the latter explanation seems more likely. Regardless of who designed the interior, it was brilliantly executed. It was an artful continuation of the exterior's Scottish Baronial theme. Symbols of Scottish nationalism and classical ideals are skillfully woven throughout the interior.

A final note on the interior is the long-standing belief that the Joslyns bought much of the furniture in the house during their visit to the Columbian Exposition. This is doubtful, as it would make little sense for them to purchase furniture that they would need to warehouse for ten years, in the hope it would match a house not yet designed. A more likely explanation is that the Columbian Exposition was important to the castle's design and construction. The role it played was one of inspiration, and perhaps also the Joslyns' introduction to the talented individuals whose joint efforts would shape the design of their castle. In the end, both Chicago firms and local Omaha craftsmen worked together to create Lynhurst Castle.

A Tour of Lynhurst Castle

Although there have been many alterations of Lynhurst Castle's interiors since Sarah died in 1940, the first floor is essentially intact. The lower level and upper floors have not fared as well, and they have been extensively altered. With this in mind, it is well worth a look to see what remains.

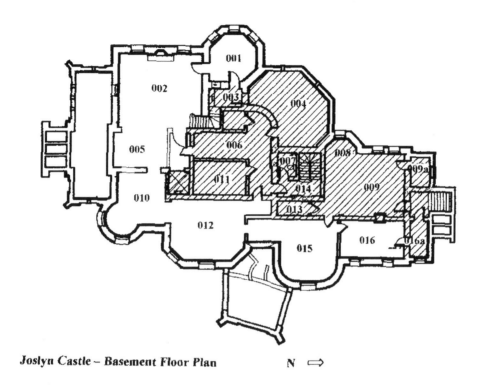

Joslyn Castle – Basement Floor Plan   N ⇨

001. Smoking Room
002. Billiard Room
003. Lavatory
004. West Cellar
005. Wine Room
006. Hall
007. Lavatory
008. Storage
009. Laundry
010. Card Room
012. Gymnasium
013. Hall
014. Stair Hall
015. Bowling Alley
016. Bowling Alley

Image courtesy of the Friends of Joslyn Castle.

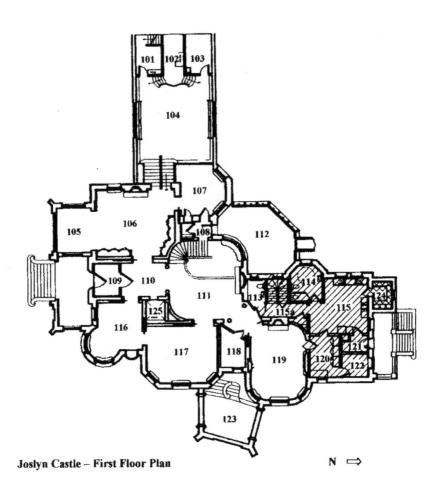

Joslyn Castle – First Floor Plan   N ⟹

101. Organ Pipes

102. Nook/Stage

103. Organ Pipes

104. Music Room

105. Sun Room/Porch

106. Library

107. Alcove

108. Hall

109. Entrance Hall

110. Reception Hall

111. Stair Hall

112. Conservatory

113. Lavatory

114. Servants' Room

115. Kitchen

116. Morning Room

117. Drawing Room

118. Entry Hall

119. Dining Room

120. Pantry

121. Servants' Entry

122. Refrigerator

123. Porte Cochere

124. Pantry

125. Closet

Image courtesy of the Friends of Joslyn Castle.

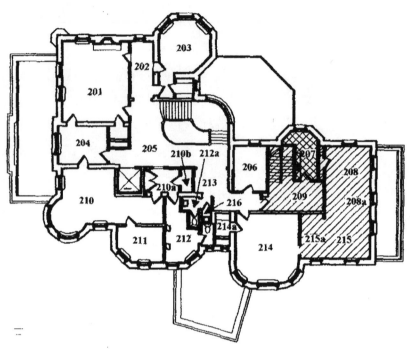

Joslyn Castle – Second Floor Plan   N ⇨

201. Guest Bedroom
202. Bathroom
203. Bedroom
204. Boudoir
205. Stair Hall
206. Bathroom
207. Store Room
208. Servant Bedroom
209. Rear Hall
210. Master Bedroom
211. Dressing Room
212. Master Bathroom
213. Staircase
214. Violet's Bedroom
215. Sewing Room
216. Entryway

Image courtesy of the Friends of Joslyn Castle.

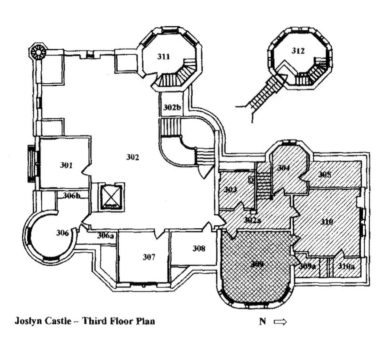

Joslyn Castle – Third Floor Plan   N ⇨

301. Bedroom
302. Ballroom
303. Lavatory
304. Servant's Room
305. Tank Room
306. Southeast Turret Room
307. Originally part of Ballroom
308. Tank Room
309. Servant's Room
310. Servant's Room
311. Northwest Turret Room
312. Fourth-Floor Turret Room

Image courtesy of the Friends of Joslyn Castle.

The Entrance Hall

Entering through the ornate 1,800-pound wrought-iron front door of the castle, the first room a visitor encounters is a small vaulted entryway, or vestibule. This space has a green and white terrazzo-tiled floor with a matte finish. The tiles are set in a geometric mosaic design mimicking a rug. The vestibule's wainscot is made of dark-green Italian marble. The walls above the wainscot are tiled with ceramic tiles. Predominantly gold in color, these tiles have a gloss finish. Two shield-shaped mosaic emblems made of brilliantly colored tiles that depict fleurs-de-lis adorn the walls of the vestibule. This floral motif is continued in a frieze of tiles depicting heart-shaped flowers directly below the marble cornice molding. The distinctive vaulted ceiling is the most interesting and attractive feature of this space. Muted gold tiles and opalescent pieces of Italian art glass on the ceiling reach to the peak of the vaulted room. The tiles and pieces of art glass form a striking mosaic pattern of abstract leaves receding up the ceiling of the vault.

The room still has its original lighting fixture, with a martial theme of shields and fleurs-de-lis. A close look at the design of the lighting fixture demonstrates that the room was designed to complement its design to create a consistent and pleasing whole. This theme is carried throughout most of the first level, with the design of the lighting fixtures appearing to dictate the design of the rooms.

Leaving the vestibule, a visitor enters the small reception area attached to the large stair hall. Both this area and the stair hall have wainscoting of Spanish mahogany. The misnamed Spanish mahogany is a hardwood that grows in the Caribbean basin on the island nations of Cuba, Haiti, the Dominican Republic, and on some islands of the Bahamas. Spanish mahogany was not named for its geographic range, but because Spain controlled the island nations where the most prized specimens of the tree grew. It is easy to see why this wood is so prized for use in paneling and furniture. It has a rich, dark-brown color with a beautiful grain pattern.

In the small reception area, an elevator occupies the east side of the room. The Omaha Public Schools installed the elevator in 1957, when the building served as their headquarters. Originally, the space occupied by the elevator was a coat closet with a large bank vault hidden behind the closet and accessed through a concealed panel. To create the space needed for the elevator shaft, contractors lowered the vault to the basement and then constructed the elevator shaft. The bank vault is still in the lower level of the castle.

Continuing through the small reception area, one notices the peaked Gothic archway leading into the large stair hall. A shield, carved in relief, is at the apex of the archway. The revival schools of architecture used many Gothic design elements, such as peaked archways. The symbolism harked back to a time when a nation's wealth and status were measured by the size and grandeur of its castles and cathedrals. Gothic arches are also carved in relief on the paneling of the stair hall's south wall.

The Great Stair Hall

The archway opens into the large stair hall. This room was originally graced with a large bearskin rug on the floor and a stuffed owl on top of the fireplace mantel. The original wallpaper in the room featured hand-painted thistles (Scotland's unofficial national flower). The most striking feature of this space is the curved grand staircase along the west wall. The staircase opens all the way to the entrance of the third-floor ballroom. This adds to the perception of increased size in the room and improves airflow in the house. The massive hexagonal newel-posts at the top and bottom of the staircase are topped with ornate carvings of acanthus plants. The acanthus is an ornamental fern native to the Mediterranean region of southern Europe. Prized for its ornate serrated leaves, it has been used in architectural decorations for centuries.

Passing the staircase, one encounters three stained-glass windows, which offer a view of the interior of the conservatory, filled with lush plantings and a tufa stone waterfall and pond. The conservatory is equipped with a band of electric lights above the waterfall that creates an enchanting effect at night. Dominating the stair hall's north wall is the grand fireplace with its ornately carved Spanish mahogany mantel and front panels of black Italian marble interspersed with gold veining. During the holidays, the Joslyns placed their Christmas tree in front of the grand fireplace.

The stair hall joins several of the rooms on the main floor with large entryways into each room. These openings make each room seem larger. This and the need for improved airflow were the reasons for the inclusion of these grand stair halls in revival designs. The large entryways posed the problem of large doors for McDonald. He overcame this problem by using pocket doors on the first floor of the mansion. The most impressive of these doors is the one leading into the drawing room, currently called the Gold Room, on the eastern side of the stair hall.

The Drawing Room

The drawing room is the most ornately decorated room in the castle. A central feature of large homes and mansions of the time, the drawing room was dedicated to welcoming important visitors and was designed to impress them. To achieve this effect, these rooms were purposely decorated in lavish and opulent styles. The castle's drawing room has exotic satinwood paneling on its wainscot. (Satinwood is a hardwood tree that grows in southern India and in the West Indies.) On its walls is a gold damask fabric wall covering that was installed in 1990. The lintels above the doorways are ornately carved with a heart-shaped egg-and-dart design. The room's ceiling and chandelier are its most distinctive features. The ceiling is composed of several different types of premolded plaster. Fabric panels with hand-painted roses and gilding further enhance the ornate ceiling. The room also has an elaborate twenty-four-karat-gold-plated crystal chandelier and two matching wall sconces. The Friends of Joslyn Castle finished restoration of the lighting fixtures and the room's ceiling in late 2005. The

Joslyns may have purchased the original furniture that graced the room at the Louisiana Purchase Exposition in Saint Louis, Missouri in 1904.[2]

The Morning Room

On the south side of the drawing room is the entryway into the morning room where Sarah spent part of her day dealing with household matters, reading her mail, and working on her charitable endeavors. This room was restored in 2003 at a cost of approximately $50,000. It is currently the only room in the home to have been restored to its original condition. The wainscot of the room is paneled in primavera wood, a tree native to Central and South America. The walls are an attractive blue, and a decorative frieze of banded foliage below the cornice molding surrounds the room. The design of the frieze closely resembles that of the room's two wall sconces.

Another feature of the room is stenciled bands of aluminum leaf running up the walls and above the wainscot. The use of aluminum seems unimpressive today. However, at the time of the mansion's construction, aluminum was a very expensive material that cost as much as gold or platinum. The cornice molding is made of painted pre-molded plaster sections depicting two classical motifs. The upper design of oval and arrow shapes is referred to as egg-and-dart. The ancient Greeks used it to decorate their temples. It signifies the course of life, with the egg representing the beginning of life and the dart signifying its end. The early Christians adopted this motif and incorporated it into the design of many churches and cathedrals. The motif below the egg-and-dart is known as a dentil, due to its resemblance to a row of teeth. The Greeks also used this molding design extensively.

The morning room was reported to have been Sarah's favorite room in the house, and she decorated the walls with pictures of their family and friends. The room's central feature is a unique flower-display window. This large bay window provides ample space for large floral displays. It is equipped with adjustable glass shelves and wire holders for vases. The window has adjustable grilles at the top and bottom that open to allow air to circulate over plants inside the window. An electric fan and a light were originally installed at the top of the window. The bottom of the window has a copper drain plate, and it is equipped with a folding faucet. On the south panel of the window, a copper-lined ice compartment is concealed behind a wooden grille. The ice helped preserve any cut floral displays Sarah installed. Below the wooden grille, a small pipe allowed water to run into the copper drain plate as the ice melted.

The Library

The entryway on the west side of the morning room leads back into the small reception hall near the front entrance of the castle. Across from this is the larger entrance into the library. The library is one of the largest rooms in the castle, and its original size was increased after the castle was completed. In 1907, the western section of the large front porch was enclosed to make a sunroom adjoining the library. Built-in cabinets with glass doors lining two walls of the room were used to display the

Joslyns' many books and artworks. The room was heavily furnished with large leather couches and an enormous library table. The woodwork in the room is Circassian walnut, prized for centuries because of its beautiful grain patterns and rich brown color. Circassian walnut is known by a variety of names, often being referred to as English or Persian walnut. The fireplace in the room is faced with Italian marble. At one time, a unique screen in the shape of a half-completed jigsaw puzzle stood in front of the fireplace. It was modeled on pieces from a jigsaw puzzle that George and Sarah had particularly enjoyed assembling. Unfortunately, the screen was lost after Sarah's death.

The sunroom on the south side of the library has a small built-in cabinet flanked by a wooden bench. Above the bench is a large and attractive art-glass window depicting wisteria vines and flowers. The window is in the Art Nouveau style and reportedly contains over 2,000 individual pieces of glass.

The ornate chandelier in the library is original, and it was designed with an oriental motif. Designs inspired by the Japanese and Chinese cultures were quite popular at the end of the nineteenth century. Their popularity reflected the public's fascination with the stories they read in newspapers of these exotic Eastern lands and their peoples.

The Music Room

On the western side of the library, a staircase leads down into the music room. This room was not part of the original structure; it was added in 1907. A building permit issued on May 7, 1907, estimated the addition's cost at $10,000.[3] The room was constructed around an Aeolian organ that George had ordered on December 31, 1906. The organ, named Opus 1035 (each organ shipped by the Aeolian company was given the designation Opus followed by the organ's individual identifying number), was shipped on June 26, 1907.[4] The original cost of the organ is unclear, but on June 23, 1908, George contracted with the company for a series of additions and improvements to his organ. These improvements cost George $10,000. (Adjusted for inflation, the amount spent on improvements alone equals about $188,000.)[5] Prior to adding the music room, the Joslyns had a piano and a Pianola in the morning room. A Pianola was a compact version of a player piano that operated automatically by playing perforated paper sheets or punched metal disks.

The new organ was a technological wonder. Instead of being operated mechanically, it was controlled by a complex series of electromechanical switches. This allowed the organ's pipes to be placed anywhere in the structure. At Lynhurst, the major pipes were located behind the grillwork on the west wall of the music room. Smaller pipes were located behind grilles on the east side of the room and perhaps even under the stairs leading down from the library. There were also pipes installed in an alcove of the third-floor ballroom, effectively making the entire mansion a pipe organ.

In addition to this unusual and complex series of pipes, the organ had other unique features. Chief among these was that it could be operated with perforated paper scrolls similar to those used by Pianolas. These were much more complex than the scrolls used by the much smaller Pianolas; they allowed the organs to replicate whole symphonies. The Aeolian company hired several noted composers, such as Camille Saint-Saens and Victor Herbert, to write compositions exclusively for use with their organs.[6] The use of the scrolls also allowed someone with limited musical training to easily operate the complex organ like a master musician. George would often delight in using this feature to entertain and impress his guests, personally performing impromptu concerts for them. The music room became the heart of the castle, and George hired world-famous organists to come and play his organ.

Although the organ has long since been removed, first to the Joslyn Memorial and later to a small university, the music room is still a very beautiful and intriguing space. The north and south walls each hold opposing banks of three tall art-glass windows. These six windows, depicting stylized white roses and lyres, are designed in a different style from the other art-glass windows in the house. They closely resemble art-glass windows designed by architects of the Prairie school. The style began in Chicago around 1900 and was championed by noted architect Frank Lloyd Wright. It was a reaction to the dark, confined interiors and imposing exteriors of the heavy revivalist structures. Its proponents sought to make interiors more open. They used banks of large art-glass windows to provide more light to the interiors of the houses they designed. The colored glass and the opaque panels used in the windows filtered and enhanced the natural light entering through them. Wright referred to these windows as "light screens."

The Linden Glass Company became one of the finest producers of this style of art-glass window, and produced hundreds of Prairie-style windows. That the castle's windows bear a strong resemblance to those designed by Wright is not surprising. In 1907, the Linden Company had an extremely close relationship with Wright, and they had manufactured the windows for at least eight Wright houses. These include such famous Wright structures as the Coonley, Dana, and Robie houses.[7] The windows on the north and south walls of the music room are consistent in quality and design with the types of windows Linden was creating at the time.

These windows elegantly reflect classical and Scottish themes. The "little white rose" is a symbol of the Scottish nationalism that inspired Scottish Baronial architects. Perhaps the most intriguing decoration on the windows is the lyre, or harp. It may symbolize the harp of Aeolus, a garden novelty of the time, where the breezes would vibrate the strings. (Aeolus was the Greek god of the wind, and the inspiration for the names of both the Aeolian company and the harp.) In the late nineteenth century, several American transcendentalist authors adopted the Aeolian harp, or lyre, as a literary device for expressing the purity of the natural world. This symbolism is entirely appropriate for a room that housed George's Aeolian organ.

Prairie elements are also reflected in the cornice moldings of the music room. They are simpler and cleaner in design than the more elaborate moldings visible in the library. The scroll and dentil moldings in the music room are abstract and geometric, as opposed to the elaborately carved scrolls in the library. The built-in benches along the walls and the more understated satinwood paneling of the music room are also consistent with the Prairie aesthetic.

On the western side of the music room, there is a nook formed by the grillwork that concealed the larger organ pipes. With its raised platform, curved steps, carved railings, and art-glass window at the rear, it almost resembles a small chapel. Engineering concerns probably caused the formation of this space. Most likely, it allowed for more organ pipes while limiting the width of the room. It is a tribute to McDonald's skill that he created such an attractive space in solving a technical problem. The risers of the curved steps leading up to the space are made of fiddle-back maple, so named for the ease with which it could be worked into the curved shapes of musical instruments.

The art-glass window at the rear of the nook reportedly was George and Sarah's favorite window. The pathway, trees, and small stream depicted in the window may be an idealized version of the view from the western windows of the castle. A second theory is that the window depicts a scene from the Vermont countryside of the Joslyns' childhood. George and Sarah loved this window so much that they commissioned the artist to create a second window like it. That window is in the Joslyns' mausoleum at Forest Lawn Cemetery in northern Omaha.

Another feature of the music room is its lighting fixtures. An elegant and simple chandelier and four wall sconces light the room. A custom-made art-glass lighting fixture illuminates the staircase leading up to the library. The art-glass panel above the stairs also bears a rose motif, but it appears to be of different construction than the windows set in the north and south walls. The music room's wall sconces and chandelier also have the rose motif. Again, the design of the lighting fixtures seems to influence the design of the rest of the elements in the room.

The Alcove and Lower Level

Above the music room is a small alcove. Originally, this was a small study or den. It was set off from the library for George to use as an office. After the music room was constructed, this area was incorporated into it as a balcony. The small room has a lighting fixture with Quezal art-glass shades. Quezal was a company formed by Martin Bach Sr. in 1902, after Bach had left the studios of Louis Comfort Tiffany. Quezal was considered one of the best manufacturers of Art Nouveau art glass, and the company's lampshades are considered equal in quality and artistry to those created by Tiffany's studios.[8] This lighting fixture has the same rose pattern as the chandelier and sconces in the music room.

The alcove contains two art-glass windows. One opens into the conservatory and the other onto the northwest grounds of the estate. George reportedly had his desk situated so he could gaze out of either window while working in the room. The wainscoting of this room is painted or grained with a heavy stain. It is likely that soon after the construction of the music room, the wood in this alcove was stained to match the satinwood in the music room.

On the east side of this small room, an entryway leads back into the stair hall. Inside the entryway is a glass-paneled door leading into the conservatory, and a door opposite to it that leads into the lower level of the castle. The lower level was George's domain. It contained a billiard room, a card room, a wine cellar, a gymnasium, and a one-lane bowling alley. The billiard room had a brick fireplace and two large billiard tables. Above one table was a large mounted elk's head. In keeping with George's philosophy of regular exercise, the gymnasium was well-equipped with the latest types of electric fitness equipment. George would often take visitors on tours of the facility to show off its advanced equipment. After modifications to the lower level, the room that housed the gymnasium no longer exists. The bowling alley is located on the east side of the lower level in a long, narrow room. The alley still exists, but it is in very poor condition.

Originally, the smoking room adjoining the billiard room had three small windows on the west side, but these were covered over when the music room was added to the mansion. This room spawned one of the most enduring legends about George. The legend purported that, in pursuit of gambling, George would sneak his cronies into this room by using the steam tunnel that entered the castle from the boiler building. His fellow gamblers would knock on the north door of the boiler building and be admitted by the boiler tenders, who directed George's guests through the tunnel and into the lower level. The reason given for this subterfuge was that Sarah was vehemently opposed to George's gambling and would not knowingly allow it in her home. This story is almost certainly untrue. Entering the tunnel from the boiler-room side required climbing a fourteen-foot-tall ladder, which was no doubt covered with soot and coal dust. In addition, the tunnel is simply too small for a person to walk through without substantial risk of getting soot and grime on his clothes.

Returning to the main level, one crosses the stair hall from the small entryway to the lower level to arrive at the entrance to the dining room on the northeast side of room. In front of the entrance to the dining room, the not-quite-intersecting oval corners of the stair hall and the dining room form a small hallway. There are four entryways in this small space. The door on the east side leads into the small alcove of the porte cochere, or covered entryway, on the east side of the castle. This small alcove has a terrazzo-tiled floor. A door once led outside to the porte cochere, and there was a narrow flight of steps up to the second floor. The school system later removed the steps and replaced the outside door with a window to create a coat closet. The large entrance to the dining room, with its unique curved pocket doors, is next to this doorway. On the west side of the dining room entrance, a small swinging door led into the narrow hall once used by the servants. The final doorway on the west side is set back in an alcove and leads into a small lavatory.

Directly in front of this door is a small marble basin with its own water faucet. The Joslyns installed this whimsical basin for their dogs. They owned several purebred Saint Bernard dogs and showed them in local dog shows. Their most famous dogs were named Safford and Modjeska.[9] These dogs, a male and a female, were mated in 1892 and produced a litter of three puppies. The female dog was named after Madame Helena Modjeska, a famous Polish actress. She was renowned in the United States and had close ties to Sarah's friend Lula Belle Chase. Safford may have been named after another friend of Sarah's. Neither Safford nor Modjeska lived long enough to enjoy the marble basin; however, their puppies were possibly among the first residents of the Joslyns' castle. Later, after George had died, Sarah acquired a small Pekingese dog named Toyo as a companion.

The Dining Room

The dining room is one of the most ornately paneled rooms in the castle. It is paneled in English oak and decorated in the Jacobean style. Jacobinism was a political and cultural movement in Europe that flourished in Scotland in the seventeenth century. The movement became tied to Scottish nationalism, which is why proponents of the Scottish revival school incorporated this design style. Heavy, ornate, three-dimensional carvings depicting marine motifs and heraldic symbols were used to decorate Jacobean interiors. A fine example of Jacobean design is the carved panel depicting dolphins above the dining room fireplace. The fireplace is faced with red Nubian marble and still has its original andirons.

Other features of the dining room were the built-in cabinets with glass doors and the large, open built-in sideboard where Sarah prominently displayed her china, stemware, and silver dishes. On either side of the cabinets on the south wall are brass wall sconces. These fixtures are hybrids that could use either the outboard electric lights or the central gas jet to illuminate the room. They were installed throughout the house, and several are still in place. The purpose of the hybrid fixtures was to allow homeowners to use the more reliable and less expensive gas jet when they wished.

The two most striking decorations of the Joslyns' dining room may no longer exist. The first was a large hand-painted frieze that went around the room above the cabinets. The frieze depicted birds and plants native to the United States. The frieze is thought to have been removed during the tenure of the Omaha schools and may now be lost. Some individuals involved with the castle's restoration project believe the frieze may still be on the walls and might be concealed under other wall coverings.

The second missing item is the large bowl-shaped chandelier that hung in the center of the dining room ceiling. The chandelier was made of art-glass panels and brass topped with opaque glass globes. It was approximately twenty inches in diameter and fourteen inches deep. Designed exclusively for the room, it was installed by the F. M. Russell Company of Omaha. Fremont M. Russell was also responsible for creating the ornate silver candelabra that graced the Nebraska building at the 1893 Columbian Exposition.[10] The dining room chandelier took eighteen months to make and was not ready to install until late December 1904.[11] It was reportedly removed prior to 1944 and is now feared lost.

The Servants' Area

On the north wall of the dining room, a door leads into a pantry and the servants' area of the mansion. The kitchen, linen-storage room, pantry, and walk-in cooler originally took up the rest of the first floor. Although it is inside the castle's exterior, this area was considered a separate structure and was constructed using less expensive materials. The servants used these areas as they performed their various tasks. Dividing the structure into two sections allowed the servants to go about their jobs without interfering with the family's activities. This was common in mansions of the time, when it took several servants to keep a large home operating. The servants had their own staircase, allowing them access to the upper and lower floors without having to use the grand staircase in the front of the house. The servants' staircase is located in the small hallway on the south side of the kitchen. The stairway's narrow width served as a safety precaution. If a servant stumbled on the steps, she could brace herself between the narrow walls and check her fall.

The Upper Floors

The narrow servants' staircase leads up to the rear hallway on the second floor. A long hallway leads into the family section of the second floor. On the west side of the hallway is the landing of the grand staircase. Two beautiful art-glass windows depicting thistles, reflecting the Scottish Baronial theme, adorn the space. The rest of the second floor consisted of four bedrooms for the Joslyns and their guests and two bedrooms in the rear for female servants. There were originally three bathrooms on the second floor. The largest bedroom is located in the southwest corner of the second floor. It has an ornate plaster cornice molding and is the only bedroom with a fireplace. This bedroom was normally reserved for guests of the Joslyns, but both Sarah and Violet preferred to use it when George was absent during his frequent business trips. This bedroom is adjoined to the master bedroom by a small boudoir decorated with cherrywood shelves. The wainscot of this room is made of an early laminated wall covering called Lincrusta.

The master bedroom was substantially altered during the installation of the elevator in the structure. Its entryway was moved, and the space needed for the elevator shaft took up a large portion of the room's original floor plan. The master bedroom had an attached dressing room that led into the master bathroom. The master bathroom was a large space containing two large washbasins, a sauna, a unique shower with six showerheads, and an ornate tub. It was also substantially altered by the school system.

The other large bedroom on the east side of the second floor is the only bedroom that retains its built-in closet intact. This bedroom, known as Violet's room, has molding and doors made of bird's-eye maple. Its large windows provide excellent views of the east grounds of the estate. There is one other small bedroom in the family's portion of the second floor, located on the west side of the castle. The two servants' bedrooms that existed on the rear of the second floor were remodeled after Sarah's death to create one large space.

The third floor of the house held the ballroom, a small bathroom, and bedrooms for female servants. Contrary to the belief that the ballroom was only used twice (once for Violet's debut, and a second time to host her wedding reception), it appears that George and Sarah hosted several events in the ballroom. The ballroom space has been extensively modified. On the west side of the ballroom, there is an entryway to the west turret. A staircase in this room leads to a second small room on the fourth floor. Here, stairs lead to the roof of the turret, and another doorway allows access to a small walkway on top of the castle's roof. This room was a favorite of Violet's twins, and George and Sarah enjoyed the room in the summer months when the windows and doors of the room could be opened to allow in the cool evening breezes.

This photograph provides a detailed view of the beautiful and intricate tiling in the entry alcove. Photograph by author.

The stair hall decorated for Christmas; on the left are the three art-glass windows that open into the conservatory. Photograph by author.

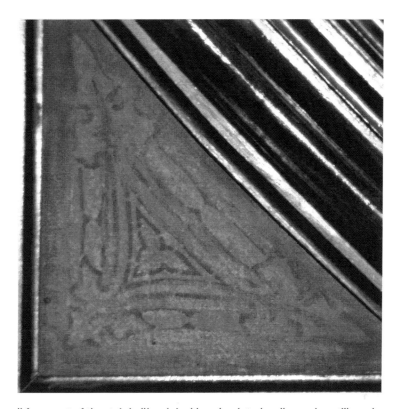

One small fragment of the stair hall's original hand-painted wall covering still can be seen on the room's ceiling, protected in a small nook formed by intersecting Spanish mahogany beams. Photograph by author.

The Friends of Joslyn Castle restored the elaborate and hand-painted plasterwork on the ceiling of the drawing room in late 2005. Photograph by author.

As part of their restoration efforts, the Friends of Joslyn Castle took down the drawing room's ornate chandelier and had it disassembled. They had the framework replated in twenty-four-karat gold and had the crystal beadwork cleaned. They also had historically accurate replacement covers made for the sconce portions of the lighting fixture. Photograph by author.

The incredible flower-window in Sarah's morning room, with its faucet in the upright position and the access grates open. The larger grate concealed a copper-lined icebox, and the smaller grate allowed access to the faucet's handle. The small pipe that allowed water to drain into the copper-lined basin of the window is visible in the center of the photograph. Photograph by author.

A photographic portrait of Sarah Joslyn hangs above the library's Italian marble fireplace. It shows her seated on a railing of the bridge that used to span the pools located on the western side of the estate. The portrait was made from a photograph given to the Friends of Joslyn Castle by Lannie McNichols. Photograph by author.

This exquisite favrile Art Nouveau-style art-glass window depicting wisteria blossoms is set in the northern wall of the sunroom addition to the library; it is reported to contain more than 2,000 individual pieces of glass. Photograph by author.

George's music room addition. The grillwork along the western wall concealed the larger organ pipes. The small chapel-like nook in the center allowed for the installation of more pipes and probably enhanced the sound of the organ. In the back of the nook is the art-glass window said to be the couple's favorite. Photograph by author.

The northern wall of the music room, with its triptych of art-glass windows attributed to the Linden Glass Company. Linden Glass manufactured art-glass windows for several homes designed by Frank Lloyd Wright. Photograph by author.

Detail of the Aeolian harp, or lyre, in the upper section of the music room's art-glass windows. George would have appreciated this secret little pun. Photograph by author.

This elegant and well-balanced art-glass lighting fixture hangs above the steps leading from the library down into the music room. Visitors to Joslyn Castle often fail to notice this fixture. Photograph by author.

Looking back from the nook between the two banks of organ pipes, the alcove is visible on the upper left side of this photograph. The three grilles below the alcove probably concealed smaller organ pipes, as did the grillwork on the steps leading down from the library. Photograph by author.

The art-glass windows of the stair hall, as viewed through the lush plantings in the last remaining conservatory. Photograph by author.

The ornately carved Jacobean fireplace in the dining room is faced with red Italian marble.
Photograph by author.

The guest bedroom's fireplace has a richly detailed curly birch mantel and mirror frame.
Photograph by author.

Detail of one of the two lovely art-glass windows depicting thistles on the second-floor landing of Lynhurst Castle. Photograph by author.

The third-floor ballroom forlornly awaits a restoration that might be years away. On the left side of this photograph is the elevator installed by the Omaha Public School System in 1957; on the right is the alcove where the portable organ pipes were placed when they were connected to the Aeolian organ in the music room. Photograph by author.

6

Self-Imposed Exile (1904–1906)

The 1903 Nebraska Legislature

As the construction season started at Lynhurst in the spring of 1903, the Nebraska Legislature was dealing with a thorny problem. Nebraska's Twenty-Eighth Legislature convened on Tuesday, January 6, 1903. The main order of business was to craft a comprehensive revenue bill to reform the way Nebraska collected taxes, and to ensure that the state would have sufficient monies in its treasury. This proved to be a difficult and contentious problem. The legislators decided to form a special committee to hammer out the details of the bill, instead of tying up both houses of the legislature. (Initially, Nebraska's legislature was divided into a senate and a house, as in other states. The legislature was not converted into a unicameral legislature until 1934.)

In 1903, several political factions in the Nebraska Legislature advanced divergent agendas. The Populists had their roots in Nebraska, and most of their support was concentrated in the Midwestern farm states. Their goals were to reform the political and social systems in the United States. They wanted to improve the lives of farmers and workers in the country, and they promoted social welfare. They were suspicious of large corporations and the wealthy, whom they felt oppressed workers and small farmers. Populism would become one of the most successful third-party efforts in American history. Populism's brightest star, William Jennings Bryan of Nebraska, carried the Democratic and Populist banners in two presidential elections and garnered almost a third of the popular vote in one contest.

While the Populists were never a majority party in the United States, they were able to force the two major political parties in the country to adopt some of their ideas and proposals. The Democrats and Republicans who attempted to incorporate Populist principles into their respective parties were known as fusionists. In 1903, the fusionist wing of Nebraska's Republican Party was a vocal minority in the party. Republican fusionists in the Nebraska Legislature held positions on legislative matters between those of the Populist and Democratic parties and those of the legislature's staunch Republican majority.

The Democratic Party held a small percentage of seats in the legislature. The Democrats were forced to work in conjunction with the even smaller Populist and Republican fusionist blocs in order to have a voice in shaping legislation. When it came to crafting the revenue bill, the minority parties were dominated by the Republican majorities in the House and Senate.

In 1903, the Republican Party controlled over two-thirds of the seats in Nebraska's house and a like number in the Senate.[1] These majorities allowed the Republicans to dominate the legislature and ensured that the revenue bill would be crafted to further their interests. Wealthy individuals and large corporate interests controlled the Republican Party's agenda. The most powerful of these groups was the railroad lobby, represented by John N. Baldwin, an attorney for the Union Pacific Railroad. The lobby represented a group of railroad companies, who had founded and financed it to promote their interests.[2] If it can be said that the Republican Party controlled the Twenty-Eighth Legislature, it might also be said that the railroad lobby controlled the Republican Party. The lobby exerted its influence over the drafting of the revenue bill and hijacked control of the committee assigned to draft the legislation.

The power exerted by the railroads went beyond merely attempting to influence legislation. Many of the senators and representatives in the legislature worked for railroad interests. These individuals controlled the leadership positions in the legislature. Representative John H. Mockett Jr., a Burlington Railroad vice president, was named speaker of the house, and several representatives who were employees of railroad companies were named to the special committee tasked with drafting the revenue bill. Among these men were Representative James Douglas, a lawyer for the Northwestern Railroad; Representative William Thompson, an attorney for the Union Pacific; and Representative William Wilson, a physician in the employ of the Burlington Railroad.[3] From the start, these individuals and other members of the special committee worked to craft a bill that would benefit the railroads.

A coalition of Democrats, Populists, and fusionist Republicans opposed their efforts. The goal of the coalition was to force the drafting of a revenue bill that would tax companies and individuals fairly. Liberal newspapers and the lobbies representing real estate men, farmers, and other corporations supported the coalition. In early March 1903, the efforts of the coalition led to the introduction of bill HR 330. The Republican majority limited debate on the bill, and it was defeated in the Nebraska house by a vote of fifty-three to thirty-eight on March 3, 1903.[4]

After the defeat of the coalition bill, the battle lines were drawn. The debate over the revenue bill became increasingly loud and acrimonious. After fending off several bills introduced by members of the minority coalition, the Republican Party was finally able to pass a revenue bill that was acceptable to the railroad lobby. On March 20, 1903, the final revenue bill (HR 344) passed the house at six o'clock in the evening. On Friday, March 27, 1903, the bill passed the Senate and was then forwarded to Nebraska Governor John H. Mickey for his signature. With their main task completed, the

Twenty-Eighth Legislature, no doubt weary from the fight, adjourned on April 9, 1903, eight days past their allotted sixty-day session.[5]

The final bill contained 244 sections and was very favorable to the railroads. The bill would raise revenue through a new schedule of property taxes on the assets of individuals, businesses, and corporations in the state. Its most controversial provision allowed for the taxation of the assets of "line corporations" at a rate of 6 percent of the total value of the assets of these companies. The law defined these corporations as those that had a substantial amount of their investment in communication or railway lines. This definition included telegraph companies, telephone companies, and of course, railroad companies. All other corporations, companies, and individuals in the state would be taxed at a rate based on 20 percent of the total value of their assets.[6]

The corporations and individuals that did not qualify for the 6 percent rate were obviously unhappy with this provision. Many Nebraskans felt the law placed an unfair tax burden on the average citizen. The public responded with vocal opposition to the law, which would take effect on March 1, 1904. Several business groups, most notably real estate interests, challenged the new law. They brought a number of lawsuits against the legislature in an effort to change the law. One of these challenges succeeded in changing the date the law took effect to April 1, 1904, but otherwise HR 344 was left intact.[7]

George's Protest

Another provision of the law taxed interests held by Nebraska residents in foreign corporations. Foreign corporations were defined as those that had been formed in other states. George and Sarah Joslyn were affected by this provision, and George was very angry about this.

After consulting with his attorney, George met with William Fleming, the tax commissioner for Douglas County. Fleming was responsible for assessing the value of personal property held by the county residents. (Douglas County includes the city of Omaha.) George complained to the commissioner that the law had singled him out after the value of his holdings in the Western Newspaper Union had been assessed at a value of $300,000. George reported that Fleming had assured him that he was not being "singled out" and showed George a list of other residents of the county who would be affected by the tax.

After his meeting with Commissioner Fleming, George and his attorney met with the Nebraska State Equalization Board to appeal his assessed valuation. The board offered to reduce the assessed valuation of his holdings in the WNU to $200,000. George's attorney felt this was a fair offer and urged George to accept it. By his own admission, George initially accepted this proposal. He soon changed his mind and declared that he would not be a tax dodger, or "kicker." (This word may refer to an individual who moves or "kicks" his assets into an area controlled by a different taxing authority, to minimize the tax on the assets.) He decided to fight the proposed taxation of his assets. The method he chose for expressing his protest was both bizarre and controversial.

After the new revenue law took effect on April 1, 1904, the stage was set for George's confrontation with the state. On April 30, 1904, George called a press conference. He announced that he was closing his new $250,000 mansion on May 1, 1904, to protest the unjust taxation. In an overstatement of his case, he claimed, "According to the best information I have been able to obtain, I am the only man in Omaha who is taxed upon stock in a foreign corporation."[8]

George announced that he had bought a new mansion near Saratoga Springs, New York; he and Sarah would move there on May 15, 1904, and they did not intend to ever return to Omaha. When asked about the fate of his Omaha mansion, he promised that he would merely close it for the summer. He added, "If my wife is contented in Saratoga, the house here will be torn down and removed and the grounds cut up into city lots."[9]

That evening, after his announcement, George and Sarah hosted a dinner party for sixteen friends at the Omaha Country Club. It is not too difficult to imagine the main topic of conversation at the table. During the next two weeks, George carried out his threat and closed Lynhurst. Shortly before their scheduled departure, George ordered two Winton touring cars from an Omaha dealer. He instructed him to ship the cars to his new estate in New York. These were the first automobiles he ever owned.

On May 20, 1904, the *Omaha Daily News* reported in a front-page story that George had instructed his head gardener, Isaac Roman, to turn two Jersey dairy cows loose to graze on the vast lawns of his Omaha estate. Roman told the reporter that the cows had been running short of feed and that George had instructed him that he could allow them to graze on the lawn. The reason for this was George's desire, as reported by Mr. Roman, to hold down expenses at the abandoned property. Mr. Roman concluded the interview by observing, "The cows are getting fat and doing nicely, and I guess I'll just keep them in there."[10]

George may have had an ulterior motive for instructing his gardener to turn the cows loose. During the final negotiations over the 1903 Revenue Act, the farmers' lobby won some concessions. Several of these dealt with exempting certain types of livestock from taxation. The broad classes of livestock exempted were animals that were not being raised for sale and all animals that were less than six months old.[11] By turning loose dairy cows, which were most likely exempt from the new property taxes, George could further make his displeasure with the new law known.

Regardless of his cows' status, George's next act of protest was his most controversial. On June 5, 1903, George issued a statement through the *New York Herald* and the *Chicago Chronicle*. It was a broadside against the Nebraska Legislature and the new revenue bill. It cataloged his objections to the bill and listed his demands if the state wished him to return. On June 6, 1903, several more large newspapers ran George's statement. The *Omaha Daily News* carried George's statement on its front page. People in Nebraska and the residents of Omaha were mortified when they read the statement and realized the negative publicity they were receiving. Below is George's statement in its entirety.

(The words or spaces in parentheses were difficult to read or unreadable in the copy of the article available.)

Unless the Nebraska legislature shall (annul) the absurd and unjust personal taxation law passed at its last session, or unless officials charged with its execution shall do so with fairness and impartiality, I will not only never again have my residence within the boundaries of that state, but I will abandon and dismantle my home in the city of Omaha, which cost me more than $500,000, and have it stand as a silent and permanent (protest) against the injustice and persecution to which I have been subjected. This is purely a question of principle with me, and the money side of it does not enter into the matter at all. In fact, the amount of personal taxation to which I object is only some $1,400, while the tax I shall have to pay on the abandoned (property) will reach from $8,000 to $10,000 a year. Of course I could sell the property if I desired to do so, as there is no lack of would be purchasers. I have already received many letters of inquiry as to what price I would accept for my place, (but) I will not entertain any offer. Never during my lifetime or that of my wife, for she is in thorough accord with my position, will I sell my Omaha residence. Situated as it is in the most attractive residence section of the city, I shall let it stand empty and neglected, and to every stranger to whom are being shown the beauties of the city the story of the abominable (…) to which I have been subjected must be told in explanation of its condition.

Please understand that I am not a tax dodger, nor a 'kicker'. During the twenty-four years that Omaha has been my home I have never made any complaint whatever about the taxes assessed against me. On the contrary, I have always been among the first to sign any petition in favor of public improvements in my neighborhood, no matter how much might thereby be added to my taxes.

The 'mystery' of my present grievance is soon told. As a result, I understand, of a long fight between the local Real Estate association and the railroads the Nebraska legislature at its last session enacted a law placing upon the tax roll all stock held by residents of that state in corporations organized under the laws of other states. Being a businessman and not a politician, I paid no attention to this bill, either before its introduction or during its progress in the legislature, and gave no thought as to what might result from its practical workings. Of course, if I had understood the real purpose of this unjust measure I should have protested against its enactment. The first I knew of its scope and intention was when I found, to my astonishment, that in addition to the usual assessment against my real and personal property in the state of Nebraska and I wish to make it perfectly plain that so far as this was concerned I have no complaint to enter I was called upon to pay taxes upon $300,000 invested in the Western Newspaper Union.

Why the amount was set at $300,000 I am at a loss to understand, for if it was right to tax it at all it surely should have (been) taxed at $1,500,000, which is far nearer its full value. This tax seemed both unjust and absurd, for it was assessed on tangible property already paying (…) taxes in half a dozen different states.

The Western Newspaper Union is not in the true meaning of the term a stock company at all. When I organized it in the state of Illinois I selected that form merely as a matter of convenience, as there are practically no other stockholders except myself, though I have given an interest in the profits to my managers in different states.

Still although this extra tax was clearly unjust, I should have paid it without any further protest than a frank and forcible expression of my opinion, had I not discovered that, for some unknown reason, I had been singled out as the only one of dozens of wealthy stock-holders with holdings in property outside of Nebraska as a victim to be (…) by the tax-gatherer.

I lost no time in calling upon the tax commissioner, William Fleming and asking him why I was the only one of the large holders of outside investments that had been assessed on such holdings. In his attempted explanation Mr. Fleming prepared for me a list of possibly 150 names of parties similarly assessed under the new law. They were all small-fry being assessed on from $5,000 to $15,000 worth of stock, all of the large fish, except myself, being allowed to slip through the tax commissioner's net entirely.

Among the names was that of a man with whose circumstances I was well acquainted. I said to Mr. Fleming:

'You claim that you are impartially (enforcing) this law. Can you tell me why you have assessed Mr. _____ on $10,000 of worthless wildcat mining stock and have entirely overlooked Mr. _____ with his large holdings in foreign stock (…)?' The only answer I could obtain to this question was a vague assurance that the tax commissioner was obliged to proceed step by step and that matters would be adjusted in time. Obtaining no satisfaction from Mr. Fleming, on the advice of my counsel I appealed to the board of equalization. After consultation they offered to reduce my assessment from $300,000 to $200,000, if I would agree not to involve them in any legal proceedings. My lawyer advised me to accept this offer in order to avoid a long and costly lawsuit, and I did so. The plan proposed by my attorney was to pay the tax on $100,000 this year and then by simply changing my business from a stock company to one of personal ownership avoid any taxes upon it in the future. At first I agreed to this as the simplest way out, but on thinking the matter over such a course seemed too much like dodging to suit me, for as I have said, it was not the amount of money involved, but the principle, and especially the injustice of singling me out as the sole victim that I objected to. And the more I thought it over the more determined I became to never give in, but to show my opinion of the treatment I had been subjected to in some practical and tangible way.

I shall pay the tax before it is due, which will be July 1, but have boarded over the windows of my residence and the cows have been turned loose on the grounds. I have recently purchased a delightful site on the western shore of Saratoga lake and shall make it my permanent home. Eventually, I may sell part of the extensive grounds of my Omaha place, but I would rather tear down the house stone by stone than abandon my silent protest against unjust and discriminating taxation.[12]

George's statement may appear on the surface to be an extreme overreaction to the situation; however, it was really a clever and elegant indictment of the legislature and its railroad masters. George indicated this when he claimed that his protest was not about money and that he was not a tax dodger. He stated several times that he was willing to pay his fair share of taxes; it was only that they were being unfairly applied that led him to protest the law. Near the end of his statement, he added that the reason he could not follow his lawyer's advice was that it struck him as unethical.

Further, George claimed that when Commissioner Fleming had shown him a list of names of other individuals who would be affected by the new tax, he had asked the commissioner why a name was missing from the list. If George had truly pointed out a name of someone who was being overlooked, it is likely that Fleming would have mentioned this in later interviews. He did not and, instead, continued to maintain that George simply did not understand that he was being treated fairly and that he (Fleming) believed George was merely being obstinate.

Some of George's other assertions in his statement are further evidence of his intent. His statement that he was unaware of the law until after the legislature passed it seems highly suspect. The contentious 1903 legislative session had received a huge volume of press coverage. His observation that he did not understand why his assets would be valued at $300,000 instead of at their true value of $1,500,000 was a direct swipe at the 20 percent valuation rate for his type of corporate assets, as opposed to the 6 percent the railroads paid. He emphasized this by claiming that the passage of the unfair law was the result of a fight between the railroads and Omaha real estate interests. When he made the claim that the "big fish" would escape without paying their fair share, there was little doubt as to whom he meant.

These were not the ravings of a deluded, wealthy man. His statement was an indictment of the railroads and of their use of their powerful lobby to win unfair concessions from the legislature. In stressing this, he implied that those who shirked their tax responsibilities were, at best, greedy and, at worst, disloyal to their community and state.

Regardless of why he made such a public pronouncement, there is scant evidence that he intended to carry out his threats. Even though he and Sarah promptly moved to their new home on Lake Saratoga, work continued at Lynhurst. The best evidence of his intention to return and occupy his new home in Omaha was that he allowed work to continue on the dining room chandelier. The custom-built chandelier was not completed until late December 1904, after taking well over a year to make. It must have been a very expensive lighting fixture. If he were not returning, he probably would have had it installed in his Saratoga home or canceled the order for it.

George and Sarah had been taking prolonged trips to Saratoga Springs, New York for several years. Their first recorded visit was a stay at the city's Grand Union Hotel in the summer of 1894. In 1895, the Joslyns also spent their summer at Saratoga Springs, during the period when they had supposedly moved to Chicago. Between 1895 and 1904, they traveled to the area several more times. It is possible that George had always intended to buy a summer home on the lake, and that he incorporated his plans into his silent protest.

The home they bought near the lake was a large, wooden, two-story structure surrounded by a porch and topped with a third-floor cupola. Soon after they moved to Lake Saratoga, George bought a thirty-foot-long, steam-driven launch. He enjoyed sailing on the lake and driving his new automobiles.[13] On June 26, 1904, the *New York Times* reported that George had renamed his home "Camp Bord du Lac;" it had been formerly known as "Shore Inn."[14] During a visit to Omaha in mid-July, George was reported to be "looking well, bronzed indeed by his exposure to the sun while automobiling in the vicinity of his new home or sailing in his steam launch on beautiful Lake Saratoga."[15]

In Omaha, meanwhile, few appreciated the subtleties of George's protest. At a meeting of the Omaha Real Estate Board in early June, the members voted down a motion to discuss George's protest, issuing a statement that it would be beneath their dignity to do so.[16] In early July, the mayor of Omaha and the Omaha City Council threatened to condemn the Lynhurst estate. They vowed to tear down the mansion and place a road through the center of the property if George did not come to his senses and return.[17]

Omaha newspapers were strangely quiet about the controversy. The heavily Republican-leaning *Omaha Bee* virtually ignored the story. The Democrat-leaning *Omaha World-Herald* covered it briefly. The more independent *Omaha Daily News* reported on the story as it progressed and was the only Omaha newspaper to carry George's statement. Only the weekly *Omaha Excelsior*, edited by Clement Chase, seemed to delight in the story. (Chase was a frequent critic of Edward Rosewater, the publisher of the *Omaha Bee*.) His paper offered several stories about the dispute and George's exploits at his new home on Lake Saratoga.

After the initial furor, the whole incident seemed to die a quiet death. George returned in November 1904 to open Lynhurst for the holidays, and the talk of retribution against him died down. In 1905, he returned to Lake Saratoga for the summer, but he and Sarah were often in Omaha. In 1906, George (who had become an automobile fanatic) purchased a new $8,000 Hotchkiss touring car to use while in Omaha.[18] He and Sarah began to be mentioned more frequently in Omaha society columns. Throughout the period of the Joslyns' self-imposed exile, they never seem to completely abandon Omaha. By early 1907, the dispute appeared to be all but forgotten, and George and Sarah were once more at the center of the Omaha social set.

However, the issues that initially sparked the dispute lasted much longer. In 1920, Nebraska held a constitutional convention; it changed the 1903 valuation formula and dropped the 20 percent valuation in favor of valuations based on the full value of property.[19] The railroads continued to enjoy their special status until 1960, when a group of railroad companies lost an appeal of a 1959 revenue bill, which had revoked the lower assessment rate.[20] The law taxing foreign corporations was the subject of several lawsuits that questioned its constitutionality. All were decided in favor of the state, the last challenge being *Rehkopf v. Board of Equalization* in 1966.[21] The descendants of George's Jersey cows have fared much better, and currently all livestock in Nebraska is exempt from property taxes.[22]

7

The Social Whirl (1907–1912)

S. Archer Gibson

In early 1907, George and Sarah decided to add a large music room to their mansion. The details of this room and its Aeolian organ were discussed in Chapter 5. Their new music room became the social center not only of their house, but also of the entire city. The room and its organ are first mentioned in late 1907, when Sarah opened her house to entertain twenty-five visiting "maids" of Ak-sar-ben (Nebraska spelled backward). These young women were in Omaha to attend the October coronation of the new king and queen of Ak-sar-ben's Kingdom of Quivira, a mythical kingdom rumored to have once existed in the area that would later become the states of Nebraska and Kansas. Spanish explorer Francisco Coronado searched for it in vain in 1541. A group of prominent Omaha men formed the Ak-sar-ben organization in 1895, and the organization continues to hold this event each year. The group recognizes the civic efforts of a leading businessman or civic leader by declaring him honorary king. The queen is selected from the ranks of the daughters of Omaha families, again as recognition of that family's civic contributions. The maids of the court are the daughters of prominent Nebraska families.

Shortly after they installed the organ, the Joslyns began hiring professional musicians to perform for them. The first organ recital held in the home took place in early December 1907, during a large party and dance given by the Joslyns for the Dallie sisters, who were visiting from Montreal. There is no record of the name of the organist who performed at this event. The first professional organist known to have played the organ was Frank Simms, who performed for the Tuesday Musicale Club on January 7, 1908.[1] Simms was the organist and music director at All Saints Church in Omaha. The next professional musician to play the organ was Frank Taft, a noted organist from New York. Taft performed on the evenings of Thursday, November 12 and Friday, November 13, 1908. George and

Sarah invited about fifty guests to each recital. After Taft's performances, the guests were served refreshments and had an opportunity to meet the artist.[2]

In 1909, George had the organ substantially enlarged and invited S. Archer Gibson to perform a series of recitals at Lynhurst. Gibson arrived in late April 1909 and stayed with George and Sarah for five weeks. Archer Gibson was an extremely gifted musician, and he only performed for the wealthiest and most prominent families. Besides playing for the Joslyns, he was a guest organist at the homes of Andrew Carnegie, Louis Comfort Tiffany, John D. Rockefeller, and a host of other wealthy families.

Gibson was born on December 15, 1875, in Baltimore. His parents were both gifted musicians. He showed remarkable musical aptitude, and by the age of ten he was giving organ recitals at a local church. He attended New York's City College and later taught at the Peabody Conservatory. He was made a fellow of the American Guild of Organists in 1902. He served as organist at the Brick Presbyterian Church in New York City from 1901 until 1909.

Gibson was dissatisfied with his position at the church. He did not like performing at church services and felt that being confined to liturgical music stifled his talent. He was also unhappy with his meager income, and his flamboyant personality made him a poor fit in the role of a church organist.

Although married, Gibson had a series of romantic trysts with young women. As his relationship with the church's pastor soured, he would often annoy the pastor by displaying pictures of his young paramours in the organ loft.[3] In 1909, after Gibson began an affair with Mary Jungten, a married female soloist at the church, he was dismissed from his position.[4] An unrepentant Gibson would later say of his replacement, "Clarence Dickinson is a virtuous organist; I am an organ virtuoso!"[5]

His dismissal placed him in a quandary. No matter how talented he was, his résumé did not lend itself to finding employment with another church. By this time he had already performed several times for wealthy families in the New York area, and he had been paid well for these performances. He began to solicit his wealthy patrons for positions as a house organist. This career choice proved to be so successful that Gibson became one of the wealthiest musicians of his era. By 1909, he was also associated with the Aeolian Organ Company. The company asked Gibson to make several perforated recordings for them. He recorded seventy-two compositions for the company, more than any other artist.[6] It may have been his association with the company that brought him to the attention of George Joslyn.

Gibson could be a difficult person. He would only perform on organs that he felt were worthy of his great talent; therefore, his wealthy patrons considered it a great social coup to have Gibson as their "guest." He would generally remain at a patron's home for several weeks. Upon leaving, he would give his patrons a "souvenir program" of their time together. The program would list his performances and some of the musical compositions he had performed. It might also mention any highlights of the visit. At the bottom of the program there would be a discreet figure listed, a subtle reminder to Gibson's patron of the amount they had agreed on as Gibson's fee. (His average fee was $175 for each recital he gave.) Each year at Christmas, Gibson would send his patrons flowers.[7]

His first visit to Lynhurst was his longest, and he gave his last performance at the mansion on Sunday evening, May 30, 1909. During this stay, he performed several recitals in the music room. He also gave one benefit concert at a nearby Baptist church. During his first stay at Lynhurst, he performed before a total of five hundred guests in the music room.[8]

Gibson created a sensation in Omaha society. He was tall and always fashionably dressed, with wavy, dark hair and long, slender fingers. With his good looks and his refined demeanor, he appeared the very ideal of a musical genius. The *Omaha Excelsior* commented on Gibson's appearance during a later visit: "At his recitals Mr. Gibson appears in a handsome black velvet sack coat, something like a tuxedo, only not, and affects a black stock, which with his jet black hair brushed firmly back and the round tortoise shell eyeglasses that are now so much in vogue with their black ribbon attachment, gives him an appearance very distingué."[9]

During his 1909 visit, Gibson allowed a telephone connection to be placed in the music room. Casper Yost, the president of the Nebraska Telephone Company, installed a private telephone line running from a microphone on the balcony of the music room to the bedside of Dr. Harry Lyman, four blocks away. Dr. Lyman was the son of George and Sarah's friends, Mr. and Mrs. Charles Lyman. He had been hurt in a carriage accident and had been bedridden for several years. The Lymans had requested the phone line so that their son might enjoy Gibson's performances. In a later article about the phone connection, the reporter noted that "the sound came through so clearly that he (Dr. Lyman) could hear the parakeets singing near the conservatory."[10]

Gibson would visit Lynhurst at least three more times. In 1910, he came for a brief visit, with his new bride in tow. He had interrupted their honeymoon to perform at a benefit concert that Sarah had arranged. (The new Mrs. Gibson was the same Mrs. Mary Jungten whose affair with Gibson led to his forced resignation from the Brick Church.)[11] In 1913, Gibson, who was noted for scrupulously following his performance schedule, arrived in early May, less than six weeks after a massive tornado had struck Omaha, badly damaging the Joslyns' home. Fortunately, the organ had survived unscathed.

During his visits to Omaha, Gibson was feted by local society. He would often attend events as George and Sarah's guest. He was a favorite of Omaha's society-page editors, and he gave several interviews during his stays. His final visit to the estate was an extended stay he made during the spring of 1914. During this visit, Sarah asked him to perform a series of concerts for groups of teachers, nurses, and social workers. He even gave one concert for the Omaha press corps.[12]

The Baron's Visit

In 1909, the Association of Commercial Clubs of the Pacific Coast invited the Japanese government to send a high-level trade delegation to tour the United States. The group had sent a delegation to Japan the year before and had suggested that the Japanese reciprocate by sending a trade delegation to the United States. The purpose of the mission was to meet with American businessmen and government leaders to discuss the potential of expanded trade between the two nations. The Japanese government quickly accepted the offer and assembled a group of Japan's most respected businessmen and diplomats.

Japan's readiness to send the trade delegation was motivated by a desire to defuse the strong and rapidly growing anti-Asian and anti-Japanese sentiment then prevalent in the Western United States. Several Western states had passed laws restricting further immigration from Asian nations. Other states had also passed laws that curtailed the legal status and rights of those of Asian ancestry who were already in America. Foremost among these were efforts to deny people of Asian ancestry the right to own property and to forbid them from becoming citizens of the United States.[13]

Americans were worried about the growing tensions with Japan for a different reason. The Japanese navy had recently inflicted severe damage to the Russian fleet during the Russo-Japanese conflict of 1904–1905. Many Americans felt there was a very real threat of an economically devastating war between the United States and Japan. The governments of both nations wanted to avoid war if possible. To ensure the success of the trade delegation, the Japanese government asked Baron Shibusawa Ei'ichi to lead it.

Baron Shibusawa was considered the eighth richest man in the world, and he was a well-respected figure in Japan. A brilliant businessman and political figure, he was credited with modernizing both the Japanese economy and the government. The baron was a visionary; he felt it was important for Japan to avoid becoming embroiled in another war. He believed the best way to achieve this goal was to create stronger economic ties with other nations and foster harmony through international trade. Sadly, his views did not prevail. He died in 1931 at the age of ninety-one. Today, the Shibusawa Ei'ichi Memorial Foundation in Tokyo continues to champion his ideals.[14]

Kokichi Midzuno, the Japanese consul general in New York, and Kazuo Matsubara, the consul from Chicago, accompanied Baron Shibusawa on his mission. Consul General Midzuno had recently arranged a gift of 3,000 cherry trees from the city of Tokyo to the people of the United States. The gift was presented at the suggestion of Helen Taft, the wife of President William Howard Taft. The descendants of the original trees still grace the tidal basin in Washington, DC.[15]

The delegation arrived in Seattle on September 1, 1909, and began a three-month whirlwind tour of the country.[16] In early November 1909, they were returning to Seattle. From there, they would sail to Japan on November 30, 1909.[17] Their mission had been a huge success. They had met with government and business leaders all over America. Thomas Alva Edison had arranged for the delegation to visit his research facilities in New Jersey; he was so impressed with the baron and his party that he visited Japan at the baron's invitation in 1911. One of the delegation's last stops had been Washington, DC. There they had met with President Taft and members of his administration.

The route the delegation's train took to Seattle passed through Omaha. Omaha businessmen and civic leaders were determined to make a good impression on the members of the delegation. They had planned a series of events, both to entertain their visitors and to inform them about Omaha.

The delegation's train slowly pulled into Omaha's Burlington Station at around nine in the morning on Saturday, November 13, 1909. It was the delegation's forty-second stop in seventy-four days.[18] The Nebraska delegation, led by Nebraska Governor Ashton Shallenberger, Omaha mayor James Dahlman, and Colonel William F. Cody (Buffalo Bill) stood on the platform, waiting to greet the baron and his party. It began raining as the delegation and their hosts exited the depot at 9:30 AM. The baron apologized, saying that he was afraid that his delegation had brought the rain with them. He was relieved when his translator informed him that the governor considered this a good omen.[19] After this brief exchange of pleasantries, the delegation split into two groups. Baron Shibusawa and the male delegates began a tour of Omaha businesses and factories. The female members of the delegation were escorted by a group of prominent Omaha women on a tour of the city's cultural landmarks. The women were entertained and feted at a series of events during the day. First the Japanese women were escorted to the home of Mrs. Gould Dietz for breakfast, and then went on to Miss Jessie Millard's home for a reception.

The proposed schedule of events planned for the visiting Japanese proved to be overly ambitious, and by midday, several events that had been planned for the visiting women were canceled. Mrs. F. L. Haller was to have hosted a tea at the Lininger Art Gallery. After learning that her event had been canceled, she graciously sent the several bouquets of roses she had purchased to decorate the gallery to the delegation's train.[20]

Finally, the Omaha women and their visitors arrived at Lynhurst at about four in the afternoon. The women rested in the Joslyns' mansion, where their male counterparts would rejoin them at 4:30 PM. When they arrived at Lynhurst, Sarah took her guests on a tour of her home, the greenhouse, and the conservatories. George presided at the controls of his organ and entertained them. Baroness Shibusawa had begged off the day's events and had remained in her private railcar during the day. She rejoined the female members of the delegation at Lynhurst shortly before the baron and his party arrived.

While the women of the delegation were touring the city, the baron's party had toured Omaha's businesses and factories. They were transported about the city in a fleet of new streetcars. They first toured the Union Pacific Railroad shops north of downtown Omaha. They continued to the McKeen Motorcar Factory, an Omaha business that manufactured streetcars and had donated the new cars that transported the delegates. From there they continued to Omaha's new water-pumping station north of the city. They ended their tour at the South Omaha stockyards. Throughout the day, Colonel Cody tagged along with the party. He appears in several photographs taken during the day. They portray the tall and still-handsome Cody towering over the diminutive baron.

By the time the baron's party arrived at Lynhurst, the Japanese were exhausted. Earlier in the day, the elderly baron had fallen asleep during a conversation with Governor Shallenberger. The delegates had decided that they would cut short the visit to Lynhurst, retrieve the female delegates, and return to the train to rest; however, when the members of the baron's party arrived, the estate and its stone castle awed them. George was bombarded with questions about his home from the younger male delegates. How much did this cost? How does the organ mechanism work? Does everyone in America have a gymnasium and a bowling alley in their basement? Meanwhile, the female members of the delegation were impressed by the vast quantities of lush plants and flowers growing in the conservatories and greenhouse.

George was in his element, and he went around the house answering his guests' many questions. He implored them to enjoy his home's amenities, and played his organ to entertain them. As the time to depart neared, Consuls Midzuno and Matsubara removed the diplomatic badges from their lapels. In an elegant gesture, they presented them to Sarah and her friend Lula Belle Chase to thank them for their hospitality.[21]

Promptly at seven, the entire party assembled at the Omaha Club for a formal banquet honoring the delegates. Mr. Frank Haller, president of the club and the husband of the woman who had earlier sent her roses to the delegation's train, rose to offer a few opening remarks welcoming the visitors. After he spoke, Governor Shallenberger, General Manderson, Baron Shibusawa, and others gave a succession of toasts and speeches. The highlight of the evening came when William Jennings Bryan, Nebraska's most famous politician, rose to address the crowd.

Bryan was one of the best orators in the country. He is best remembered for his famous "Cross of Gold" speech, delivered at the 1896 Democratic National Convention. Bryan was popular in Japan, and his presence thrilled the members of the Japanese delegation. After Bryan's address, the Japanese and American guests at the banquet rose and cheered wildly in unison. It would later prove to be a rueful memory for some of the participants because they all cheered, "Rah! Rah! Rah! America, Nippon, Nippon, Omaha, Banzai!"[22]

In May 1910, the consortium that arranged the delegation's visit issued a report. The report provided a detailed summary of all the cities visited and of the events that had occurred in each. Highlights of the visit to Omaha included meeting the famous Colonel Cody and the brief visit to Lynhurst.[23]

Violet and David

At the time of the Baron's visit, Violet was seventeen years old and had just begun her senior year in high school. As she matured into a young woman, Violet became a social butterfly. She attended many society events and began to hold her own parties at Lynhurst. She was first mentioned in the society columns as a guest at a luncheon at the Omaha Country Club in 1905, when she was thirteen years old.[24] George and Sarah took a great deal of interest in her well-being. They sent her to the best schools available. She graduated from Brownell Academy, then an exclusive school for young women, in June 1910. The summer before her graduation, George and Sarah took Violet on a grand tour of Europe for three months. During their travels, they toured all the countries in Western Europe, including Scotland.[25] After their return from Europe, the Joslyns sent Violet to the Bangs and Whiton School in New York City. She attended the school for one year, returning to Omaha in the late summer of 1911.

1911 was a busy year for Violet. In late September, she was mentioned as a potential queen of Aksar-ben. When her friend Elizabeth Davis was crowned queen, Violet served as a maid in her court. In December, Sarah held a formal tea in honor of the debuts of Violet and Helen Scobie, one of Violet's best friends. (In 1917, Helen married Alan McDonald, the son of architect John McDonald, after the younger McDonald went into partnership with his father.)[26] That evening, following the tea, the Joslyns hosted a grand ball for the young women in the mansion's third-floor ballroom. A week after the festivities, Violet and Helen accompanied the Joslyns on their annual trip to Hollywood, California. While there, the group stayed at the mansion of George's friend George Bidwell. After Violet returned from California in May 1912, she settled into the life of a wealthy young socialite. She had grown into an attractive young woman, tall and slender, with a lovely smile. She was frequently mentioned in society columns as dining at country clubs, attending theater parties, and going to large picnics held at the summer homes of her friends' parents. One of her favorite activities was going to the Metropolitan Club in downtown Omaha. She and her friends held swimming parties at the club's indoor pool and dined afterward at the club's restaurant. Violet hosted a party at the club in August 1912. She treated her guests to a dip in the pool and dinner. Afterward, she and her friends talked about forming a coed water-polo league at the club.[27]

In 1911, Violet met a young Cornell University graduate named David Magowan. He had moved to Omaha in 1911 to work for the Swift Company, a large national meat-processing firm with substantial facilities in the city. By 1912 he had been promoted by the company and was soon an assistant superintendent at one of Swift's Omaha processing plants. He must have made quite an impression on Violet. In their 1991 interview, her daughters reported that their mother had been dating another man when she met David. She broke up with this young man soon after she met David.[28] On March 12, 1913, Violet and David became engaged.[29] They announced that they would be married at Lynhurst in October.

8

Beginnings and Endings (1913–1916)

The Easter Tornado

The year 1913 began briskly for George and Sarah, with no hint of any dark clouds on the horizon. George had been ill for a brief time, but by late January, his condition had improved. Violet attended several parties in the first few months of 1913, and by late February was preparing to announce her engagement. Sarah had been elected to head the membership committee of the Omaha Fine Arts Society. She had also arranged for Violet to be secretary of the Society's junior branch. In March, Sarah was elected to the board of the Unitarian Church. By late March, the Joslyns were busy preparing for the visit of Archer Gibson, who was to arrive at the house in early May.

Easter Sunday, March 23, 1913, dawned with a lead-gray sky. The day was cold; the temperature hovered near freezing throughout the day. In the afternoon, the skies began to clear, and most residents of the city settled into their homes to find what comfort they could during the waning hours of the day. With little warning, the skies began to darken in the late afternoon, and at approximately 5:45 PM, the tenth-worst tornado in the history of the United States struck Omaha. In less than an hour, the city was devastated. Over one hundred people were dead. Hundreds more were injured, and thousands were left homeless.

The tornado first struck the southwestern edge of Omaha and the small communities of Ralston and Papillion. It proceeded northeast until it veered north on Thirty-Ninth Street and directly across the grounds of Lynhurst. After striking the estate, it continued northeast into northern Omaha and then into western Iowa. The storm left behind a seven-mile-long path of destruction in Omaha, severely damaging many areas of the city. As the storm passed through north Omaha, it completely demolished the Idlewild Club, located at Twenty-Fourth and Grant streets. The club, a pool parlor frequented by residents of the area, was believed to have had about thirty men in it when the storm struck. The next day, firemen and volunteers removed the bodies of seven men from the wreckage of the club. On the following Tuesday, six more bodies were recovered from the site. The death toll for those in the club eventually reached nineteen.[1]

A few blocks from the Idlewild, young women operators staffed a telephone exchange at Twenty-Sixth and Webster streets. When the storm struck, they were busy connecting phone calls. The storm shattered the windows of the exchange, and several of the young women were badly cut by flying glass. Nevertheless, they all bravely remained at their posts throughout the evening.[2]

Besides the horrible toll at the Idlewild, there were tragic instances of entire families killed by the storm. The storm demolished the home of Cliff Daniels, near Nineteenth and Locust streets. Daniels, his wife, and their two young daughters were found dead in the wreckage. Only their sixteen-year-old son survived.[3] The tornado destroyed the residence of the Nathan Krinski family, located at 2308 North Twenty-Fourth. He and his wife, along with their five young daughters, all perished.[4]

Only blocks from the Joslyns' estate, firefighters and neighbors worked feverishly to free Maude Hogg, who was trapped near a leaking gas pipe in the cellar of her home. The men made several attempts to reach her, but debris covering the doors and the gas leak thwarted their efforts. Maude assured them that she was not injured but that she was pinned to the floor and could not move. Several times during her ordeal, she wept and begged the men to hurry. The men tried to calm her. They looked in vain for another way into the cellar. As the cellar filled with gas, her voice grew fainter, and then she was silent. Her body was recovered from the wreckage early the next morning; she was only thirty-eight years old.[5] The following day, her husband James also succumbed to injuries he had suffered during the storm.[6]

Other areas around Lynhurst were also severely damaged by the storm. Many homes in the area were demolished, and several of the Joslyns' neighbors were severely injured. Mrs. C. E. Black and her sister (Mrs. Cotton) were badly bruised after being pinned in the wreckage of the Black home, across the street from Lynhurst. Matthew Hall, a lawyer who lived down Thirty-Ninth Street, suffered a gash in his skull.[7] Charles Pickens, a neighbor and a frequent guest at Lynhurst, had to be hospitalized for injuries and shock after his home was left in splinters.[8]

Just down the street from the Joslyn estate, Mrs. Howard Baldridge miraculously survived unharmed after being blown down the staircase of her home and out its front door. She had been preparing for a bath on the second floor of her home when the storm hit. Hearing the loud roar of the approaching tornado, she walked to the second-floor landing to see what was happening and became caught in a vortex created by the storm. Her husband found her on the front lawn, dressed in only her kimono. Mr. Baldridge, who had been in the front yard surveying the storm, reported that just as his wife landed safely on the grass, the storm struck their house. The second floor where she had been standing was totally demolished. On Monday, when the couple checked into the Loyal Hotel, Mrs. Baldridge was wearing only a gingham apron and a man's coat.[9]

Damage to the grounds of Lynhurst was extensive. Most of the windows in the greenhouse were shattered. The elegant palm conservatory was a mass of twisted metal and broken glass. The storm decimated the large orchid collection. The empty ponds were filled with debris. The stone railings of the bridge were broken and lying on their sides. George's exotic trees had been uprooted and stripped of their branches; their trunks tilted in the ground like huge wooden spears. A large limousine belonging to Nelson Updike had been flung against Lynhurst's eastern wall. (This car was initially erroneously reported as belonging to the Joslyns.)[10] Mr. Updike's driver, who was inside it at the time, emerged from the car unhurt.[11]

The Joslyns' home was also badly damaged. There was extensive damage to the roof of the structure. Much of the stonework on the turrets and chimneys had been torn off. A large pile of debris made up of stones and broken roof tiles rested on the roof of the music room. The Joslyn family and their servants survived the tornado without injuries. They had huddled in the home's library when the storm approached and fled the room amid exploding glass when the tornado struck the estate. While the exterior of the structure was intact, most of their furniture was ruined. The storm had whisked a 150-pound leather-and-mahogany chair from the library and deposited it in the Joslyns' garden, a half block east of the home.[12] In an interview a day after the storm, George told a reporter that only four rooms in the mansion were habitable. He added that the family would remain in their home.[13]

After the sun set, it began to rain heavily, and the temperature fell to below freezing. Although it made the survivors' lives miserable, the cold rain put out many of the fires caused by broken gas mains and overturned furnaces; however, these conditions made it impossible to assess the true extent of the damage caused by the storm until the next day. The next day dawned with a gray, overcast sky. A strong, bitterly cold wind blew throughout the day; Nebraska Governor John H. Morehead, during his inspection of the devastated area around Lynhurst, likened it to the roar of a satisfied lion after it had dispatched its prey.[14] As George walked among the ruins of his estate, he was heartbroken. His mansion was severely damaged, and his beautiful grounds—the pride of his life—were ruined. The Joslyns' collection of rare plants and orchids was gone. On Tuesday morning, a quiet snow began to fall, blanketing the grounds of Lynhurst like a burial shroud.[15]

The damage caused by the tornado was too much for George to bear. On March 24, in an emotional interview, he declared that it would be impossible for the couple to rebuild their estate at their age and that the effort would be too personally painful.[16] In an interview three weeks later, he said that he and Sarah would move to Hollywood. They had already purchased land near the Bidwell mansion. He added that plans for the construction of their new home were underway.[17] It does not appear that their California home was ever completed. The project is not mentioned in newspaper accounts again. After George died in 1916, Sarah appears to have abandoned the project and remained in Omaha.

Violet's Wedding

Even though George was planning to move to Hollywood, he did not intend to abandon his Omaha residence. He had hired a force of twenty workers, who had already begun to repair the castle and clear the grounds. The reason for the rapid pace of the repairs was to ready the estate for the upcoming wedding of David Magowan and Violet Joslyn. They were to be married on October 16, 1913; their wedding and reception would be held at Lynhurst.

Workmen spent most of the spring removing debris and repairing the estate's buildings. The widespread destruction caused by the tornado strained the ability of builders and architects in Omaha to cope with the rebuilding. Builders and architects from other cities assisted with the reconstruction efforts. In July, George contacted landscape architect Jens Jensen. He asked him to redesign the attached conservatory. In August, Jensen submitted his design for the conservatory. His design was of a tufa rock pond with a waterfall. After this, Jensen's direct involvement with the project appears to have ended.[18] George and Sarah decided not to rebuild the large palm conservatory. They donated what was left of the structure to the City of Omaha, along with $2,000 to pay for needed repairs. The city decided to place the palm house in Hanscom Park, located in southeast Omaha. Sarah later donated the two hundred orchids left in the Joslyn collection to the city, to place in the conservatory.[19]

By late September, the grounds of Lynhurst had been cleared, and the exterior repairs to the castle were close to completion. The glass windows of the attached conservatory were installed, and its new concrete floor had been poured. The rock pond and waterfall had not yet been started. This allowed Sarah to place the head table in the conservatory, where the bridal party was seated during the reception following the wedding.

On the evening of October 16, promptly at 8:30 PM, Mr. Ben Stanley, a local musician, began to play the Lohengrin "Wedding March." As he played, the bridal party entered the music room, where the ceremony was to take place. Reverend Thomas J. Mackay, of All Saints Church, officiated at the wedding. Reverend Mackay stood behind the railing in the small raised organ loft. The loft had been decorated from floor to ceiling with white chrysanthemums and a cross made of red roses. Several guests commented that with all the flowers and the loft's charming stained-glass window, the space resembled a chapel. More white chrysanthemums and lilies of the valley decorated the area below the loft. The organ and the niches along the staircase leading down into the room were also decorated with flowers. The grillwork enclosing the pipes of the organ had been decorated with the leaves of rare tropical ferns. The rest of the music room was decorated with green ferns and white flowers. Throughout the room, several tall white candles added their glow to the decorations.[20]

David and his best man, Thomas Lyte (a friend from David's hometown of Kane, Pennsylvania) came down the steps first. They waited for the bride and her party to descend the staircase. The groomsmen and bridesmaids entered next and took their respective places. The four bridesmaids were dressed in gowns of pale-green charmeuse with V-shaped necklines. Each bridesmaid carried a long muff, almost touching the floor, made of pink and green chiffon and decorated with pink roses. The bridesmaids also had roses entwined in their hair.

Violet appeared next at the top of the staircase, escorted by George. Together they slowly descended the stairs. Violet was dressed in an ivory-colored bridal gown of charmeuse satin with a bodice embroidered with pearls. She wore a veil of silk malines. Her gown had a long, square train, heavily embroidered with pearls and rhinestones. The train was also decorated with real orange blossoms, a gift from Mr. and Mrs. Gurdon Wattles, friends of George and Sarah who owned an estate in Hollywood, near the Bidwell mansion. The blossoms came from trees on their estate. Violet carried a large bouquet composed of orchids and lilies of the valley.[21] The organist continued to play softly during the ceremony. After the ceremony, he played the Mendelssohn "Wedding March" as the bride and groom left the music room. The wedding party adjourned to the main stair hall, where they received their guests. Sarah Joslyn was dressed in a dove gray velvet-and-chiffon gown brocaded with velvet flowers. Over this, she wore a bodice of gold-metal lace and a jade green girdle.[23] An estimated two hundred guests attended the affair.

After greeting their guests, the bridal party retired to the conservatory, where their table was decorated with white chrysanthemums, ferns, and a large bouquet of red roses. The roses were a gift to the couple from President William Howard Taft.[23] Other gifts were displayed in the third-floor ballroom. One reporter described the array of gifts in the ballroom: "The wedding gifts were tastefully arranged and where costly silver, fragile glass and Dresden ware, books, pictures, lamps of many designs, fine linen, solid mahogany were displayed in a bewildering array and gave evidence of the affection and good will of Miss Joslyn's friends."[24]

Violet's wedding was described in long, glowing accounts in all the society columns. The columnists that had attended universally considered it one of the finest social events of the year. All seemed overwhelmed by the floral decorations. The *World-Herald* columnist noted that there were beautiful floral displays everywhere in the house.[25] The only problem at the event, reported the *Daily News* columnist, was her inability to see around the large bird-of-paradise feathers that adorned the female guests' hats, and her fear of being tickled by them.[26]

After the wedding, the new couple took a five-week honeymoon. They toured the East Coast and returned on December 1. They moved into a home at 3504 Woolworth Avenue. The furnished house was their wedding gift from George and Sarah.[27] It was while living at the Woolworth address that Violet would give birth to her twin girls, Joslyn and Sally, on August 15, 1914.[28] Shortly after the birth of the twin girls, David Magowan left the Swift company and began working at the Western Newspaper Union.

George's Last Years

On November 17, 1913, George and Sarah, their niece Angie, and George and Hattie Bidwell had the Joslyns' touring car loaded onto a train, and the party left in a private car for an extended tour of the East Coast. They began with a stop in Washington, DC, and ended their tour in Miami, where they planned to spend the Christmas holidays. In January, George returned to Washington, where he had been summoned to testify before a Senate committee investigating the WNU. The investigation was prompted by allegations made by Courtland Smith of the American Press Association, during his testimony before an earlier Senate panel. While testifying about unfair competition by the WNU, Smith alleged that the WNU had accepted large payments from the Canadian government. Canada was paying the WNU to run articles that touted the richness of Canadian farmland and the economic opportunities available to Americans who emigrated to Canada.[29]

George appeared before the Senate committee on January 28, 1914. Alfred Washington, the advertising manager for the Western Newspaper Union, accompanied him. General John C. Cowin, a prominent Omaha lawyer, represented them. During his testimony, George admitted that his firm had accepted $42,000 a year for twelve years from the Canadian government.

Prior to George's testimony, the outraged senators on the committee had publicly accused the WNU management of being unpatriotic. They claimed the company was disloyal to the United States and demanded that its management explain their actions.[30] An angered George responded to their charges in an interview. He told reporters that he had nothing to explain. He pointed out that the articles were advertising and that they were printed in a different typeface to distinguish them from editorial content. George said that he could see no "earthly objection" to the advertisements.[31]

After he finished testifying before the committee, and seemingly unperturbed by the ordeal, George boarded his train and returned to his vacation. He had been correct in his assertions that there was nothing illegal about the ads, and the committee later dropped the matter. George and Sarah spent three more weeks in Florida and then headed back to Omaha.

By then, perhaps in realization of his worsening health, George had begun to focus on his legacy. He increased his charitable donations to the institutions and charities he supported. In the seven years before his death, George gave large sums to a variety of causes. In 1909, he became the major contributor to the building fund of the Child Saving Institute, pledging $25,000 to the cause. The same year, he offered Omaha University $50,000 for a new building, if the university could raise an additional $150,000 in one year. Unfortunately, the university was unable to raise the money, and his offer lapsed. In 1915, he made the school a second offer to cover half the cost of a new building if they could match his pledge of $25,000. This time their fund-raising efforts were successful, and the new building, named Joslyn Hall, was dedicated on October 25, 1916. Sadly, this was three weeks after George's death.[32]

In 1911, during a trip to his hometown of Waitsfield, George encountered Ziba McAllister, an old friend, and they discussed the need for an adequate library for the town. After McAllister jokingly pointed out that George should pay for it, he agreed.[33] In 1913, George donated over $25,000 to have the library built and to buy furniture and materials for the building. He arranged for John

McDonald to design the building. George's only stipulation was that the new library be named for his (and Sarah's) grandfather, Joseph Joslin.[34]

Unable to attend the library's dedication on October 30, 1913, George instead composed a speech to be delivered for him. In the speech, he seemed to realize that his life was almost over, and he expressed a longing to return to his boyhood home. He wrote:

> I had hoped that I might be able to meet with you today and take a personal part in the dedication of the Joseph Joslin Memorial Library Building, but circumstances which will not be reasoned with have ordered otherwise. The circumstances with which a businessman has to deal are usually hard masters; they rule him with a rod of iron and give him little heed in matters of sentiment. I have been for a long time in business servitude and my bonds are beginning to chafe. I am getting restive, but someday soon I expect to be free and then I shall come back here often to revisit the scenes of my boyhood, to breath the tonic mountain air and to meet and greet friends of other days. [35]

In April 1914, he bought five and one-half acres of land in central Omaha, which he intended to donate as the site for a new Old People's Home. After George and Sarah learned that Ida Tilden, a founder of the Home, was gravely ill and close to death, they visited the poor woman. On June 25, 1914, they presented her with the deed to the property and pledged $10,000 toward the construction of the home. Friends of Mrs. Tilden, who were present at her bedside when she died the next afternoon, reported that after the Joslyns' visit, Mrs. Tilden became calm and smiled until she passed away. Just before she died, she told them that now she could die in peace, knowing that her institution would have a new home.[36]

Besides these larger acts of philanthropy, one of George's obituaries noted that he was always ready to intervene with small personal donations for people in need. His associates at the WNU recounted that he would often carry several hundred dollars in his pocket for this purpose. If someone approached him with a worthy cause or problem, he would give them $25 or $50. The *Omaha Daily News* noted in his obituary that in the last few years of his life, he aided about six people a day in this fashion.[37]

By 1915, George's health had rapidly deteriorated. His obituaries stated that he had been in failing health for six years. This may have been related to his bout of influenza in 1908, or perhaps to his chronic cigar smoking. Even as his condition worsened, he continued to work. In 1915, George purchased two buildings in downtown Omaha. In January, he bought the Schlitz Building, located at 312–16 South Sixteenth Street. In March, he purchased the Patterson Building, located at 1623 Farnam Street. The total cost of the two transactions was $1,250,000, which he paid in cash.[38] Ironically, in view of his earlier forays into the hotel business, the Schlitz Building was the home of the Schlitz European Hotel.[39]

On April 24, 1915, George and Sarah abruptly left Omaha. They announced that they were traveling to Hollywood and would stay there for two months. While in Hollywood, they did not follow their normal routine. Instead of staying with the Bidwells, they took rooms at the Hotel Hollywood. They remained at the hotel for almost five months before returning to Omaha in early September.[40] After their return, the couple seldom attended social functions.

Sarah did, however, grant a friend's request to allow Reverend Billy Sunday to present a lecture in her music room. He spoke at 10:00 AM on Thursday, September 16, 1915. Reverend Sunday was one of the most famous evangelists of his day. Crowds adored the former professional baseball player for his plainspoken fire-and-brimstone sermons. In addition to his sermons, Reverend Sunday presented lectures about noted historical religious figures. It was this type of "drawing room" talk that he delivered at Lynhurst. Reverend Sunday was in Omaha at the time with his crusade. Although his talk at Lynhurst had been secular and educational in nature, Sarah feared that people would think that the talk had been part of his crusade. She later felt compelled to point out to a reporter that although she had allowed Reverend Sunday to use her home, it did not mean she was a supporter of his crusade. She had only let him lecture there as a favor to her friend.[41]

In early February, George made his last public appearance. He announced that he was planning to spend $440,000 on improvements to the Patterson Building.[42] Also in February, George and other Omaha businessmen signed a petition that called for the passage of an amendment in Nebraska prohibiting the sale of alcohol in the state. Several other executives of the WNU were among those who had signed the petition.[43]

George suffered a stroke in March 1916. He spent most of the last few months of his life confined to his home. A week before he died, his condition seemed to improve, and he made a last visit to the WNU headquarters, located at 510 South Fifteenth Street. On October 3, 1916, his family and associates were summoned to Lynhurst to be with him. George Joslyn died the next day at 12:43 PM. Sarah, Violet, George's sister Jennie, his close friend and associate Herbert H. Fish, and his physician, Dr. Le Roy Crummer were at his bedside.[44]

George's funeral was a private affair held at Lynhurst at 2:00 PM on Friday, October 6. At his funeral, Reverend Robert Leavens read from the Bible, and Reverend Thomas Mackay delivered George's eulogy. Reverend Mackay, who had often been a guest of the Joslyns, spoke of how George had always been there to ease the burdens of his friends. He noted that George had shared his love of music and his fine home with his friends and with the community. Mackay summed up his feelings by saying simply, "So we shall miss him."[45]

Over two hundred mourners attended George's funeral. Many of his friends and business associates from around the country came to Omaha to attend. Many prominent Omaha businessmen also attended George's funeral. As a gesture of respect for him, all work on the Old People's Home was suspended on the day of his funeral. During the service, Mr. Ben Stanley, the same musician who had performed at Violet's wedding, played some of George's favorite songs on the pipe organ. These included "Ave Maria" by Schubert, "Adoration" by Gaul, and Handel's "Largo."[46]

After the funeral, George's body was interred at Forest Lawn Cemetery in the family's mausoleum. George's obituaries praised his good works, and Reverend Mackay had delivered a laudatory eulogy at his funeral, but George's own words best express his legacy. Toward the end of the speech he had composed for the dedication of the Joseph Joslin Library, he wrote about his philosophy of giving: "I have been deeply impressed with the thought that there is, as has been often said, a genuine pleasure in judicious giving. A pleasure that leaves the giver richer by far in the essential things of life than he was before."[47]

9

Building George's Memorial
(1917–1931)

Sarah and World War I

After George's funeral, Sarah stayed in Omaha for two months. In early December, she traveled to Hollywood with her friends Mr. and Mrs. Chadwick. Coit and Angie Farnsworth also accompanied her. In April 1917, Sarah and the Farnsworths returned to Omaha. Sarah was ready to resume her life without George. While Sarah had been preoccupied with George's health, momentous events had been occurring in the world. They would have a significant and immediate impact on her life. These were the series of events that drew the European nations, and later the United States, into World War I.

On June 28, 1914, Austro-Hungarian Archduke Franz Ferdinand and his wife, Sophie, were assassinated in the Bosnian capital of Sarajevo. While there were many complex reasons that led to World War I, their assassinations are viewed as the spark that began the war. Their deaths led to demands by the Austro-Hungarian Empire for retribution against Serbia. The Empire blamed Serbia for training and arming the assassins. Through the terms of a series of interlocking treaties, the Empire's desire to punish the Serbs quickly drew the major nations of Europe into the conflict. Germany sided with the Austro-Hungarian Empire. Opposing them was a coalition of nations led by France, Russia, and Great Britain. By late August 1914, most of the nations in Europe were at war.

Although the government of the United States wished to remain neutral in the conflict, a majority of the American public supported the British and French forces. In early 1915, the German navy instituted a campaign of unrestricted submarine warfare. It announced that any Allied ship in the waters around Britain could be attacked without warning. The German government published warnings in major American newspapers, warning United States citizens to avoid traveling on these ships. On May 7, 1915, the British liner *Lusitania* was torpedoed and sunk off the Irish coast, killing 1,198 people, including 128 Americans. This atrocity, along with the sinking of the RMS *Arabic* and the RMS *Sussex*, which also cost American lives, enraged many Americans, and they urged the United States government to declare war on Germany.

The German government briefly forestalled this when it issued a formal apology to the United States. The Germans also promised to stop the unrestricted attacks. These moves placated the United States government, but by then, public opinion was so strong against Germany that young American men began to enlist in the British, French, and Canadian armies. In January 1917, a bungled plot by Germany to incite Mexico to attack the United States was discovered, and on February 1, 1917, the German navy reinstated the unrestricted submarine attacks. After the German announcement and the discovery of the Mexican plot, the American public demanded that the government act. The United States declared war on Germany and Austro-Hungary on April 6, 1917.

Patriotic fervor in the country ran high, and most Americans wanted to do all that they could to support the war effort and the young soldiers going to Europe to fight. Sarah was no exception, and she threw herself into war-related activities. She was appointed to the boards of three organizations in 1917. The first was the Nebraska chapter of the National League of Women's Services. The League was composed of patriotic women whose goal was helping the war effort.[1] In October 1917, she joined the board of the Child Saving Institute. Soon after this, in early November, she was appointed to the board of a new organization, the Omaha Association for the Protection of Boys and Girls.[2] She also was involved with the Red Cross, where she worked on a committee that arranged for box lunches to be given to departing Nebraska soldiers.[3]

In late October, David Magowan enlisted in the United States Army Balloon Corps. The Magowans sold their home on Woolworth Avenue, and Violet and her children moved to Lynhurst to live with Sarah. Violet and the children stayed with Sarah until early April. They then followed David to his new posting as a lieutenant at Taylor Field in Montgomery, Alabama.[4] In January 1918, Sarah was named third vice president of the National Humane Society.[5] Also in January, she purchased a hundred seats at the Brandeis Theater in Omaha for a patriotic show to benefit the war effort. She instructed the theater's management to distribute the tickets to the young soldiers stationed at nearby Fort Omaha.[6] On March 9, 1918, it was announced that Sarah would help oversee the third annual Liberty Loan Drive in Omaha. The loan drive was scheduled to commence on April 6, 1918.[7]

Besides all these activities, Sarah continued to stay personally involved with causes she supported. On August 5, 1918, Sarah became involved with the strange case of Margaret Anderson. Accompanied by Dr. Jennie Calfas and four other prominent Omaha women, Sarah went to the South Omaha Police Court to attend Mrs. Anderson's preliminary hearing. Mrs. Anderson was accused of shooting Joseph Reisdorff, whom she had accused of assaulting her fourteen-year-old daughter. Anderson had first accused another man of the assault of her daughter. After she discovered evidence that Reisdorff had committed the assault, she reported her suspicions to the police. The South Omaha prosecutors declined to arrest the suspect, claiming Mrs. Anderson had already named a suspect and that no one could corroborate her new story. After they failed to take any action against Reisdorff, she took matters into her own hands and shot him.

Sarah and her associates were there to show their support for Mrs. Anderson and to see that she was treated fairly by the court. In a statement to the press, Dr. Calfas said, "None of the women knew the defendant, Mrs. Anderson, but they were in court (out) of sympathy and a desire to let it be known they were ready to see exact justice be done."[8]

It is not difficult to imagine Sarah and her associates in the courtroom. They would have been dressed in ankle-length skirts and conservative hats, standing amid the petty thieves and other criminals waiting their turns at the docket. This is in stark contrast to later descriptions of her. In 1918, when she was almost seventy years old, a news account depicts her as a stouthearted defender of the rights of women and children.

Sarah also did something extraordinary: she opened her home to the young soldiers stationed in Omaha for them to use for their recreation. Sarah told a reporter, "I want the soldiers in this vicinity to know that my home and all it contains is open to them every night."[9]

The interview, held at Lynhurst, was interrupted by the arrival of a group of young soldiers. Sarah happily greeted them and gave them an impromptu tour of her home. While the young men were enjoying the amenities of the mansion, Sarah returned to the reporter. He noted that she was smiling when she told him, "I'm happy now, I only wish there were more of them here."[10]

The *Omaha Excelsior* commented on her kindness to the troops in its September 7, 1918 issue. It compared the considerations Sarah was showing these young men with those she showed her remaining horse. The horse, now twenty-three years old, was allowed to wander the estate's grounds at will. The animal was particularly fond of grazing on the grass near the greenhouse. The *Excelsior* writer referred to the horse as "Mrs. Joslyn's pensioner."[11] While the elderly horse made its rounds, the young soldiers were enjoying their off-duty hours at the estate. It is easy to imagine that these young men, alone and far from home, and generally from rural backgrounds, would have doted on the animal.

The *Excelsior's* correspondent mentioned that many of the young men had become quite fond of Sarah. Several continued to write to her after they left to fight in Europe. The reporter, who had read some of these letters, commented that they were the types of letters that "a son would write to his own mother."[12]

After the entry of the United States into the war, the situation for Germany and its allies quickly became untenable, and they were soon forced to sue for peace. World War I ended on November 11, 1918, at 11:11 AM. America's brief involvement in the war had provided Sarah with a needed distraction from her grief over the loss of her husband. For a two-year period after his death, she was involved in several war-related and charitable causes that occupied almost all of her time. With the war over, she was a wealthy woman in search of a purpose.

George's Memorial

After the war ended, Sarah dedicated her efforts toward establishing a lasting memorial to her late husband. As early as February 1919, a newspaper article mentioned her plans to establish a skyscraper in downtown Omaha.[13] It was to be dedicated to the medical profession, providing enough space to house all the physicians and other medical personnel in Omaha in one building. This project did not proceed very far. Sarah ceased her involvement in it after the effort was taken over by a group of Omaha physicians. (This building was finally built. Named the Medical Arts Building, the seventeen-story building was completed in 1927. It was demolished to make room for the First National Center in 1999.)[14]

On April 24, 1920, Sarah announced that she had decided to build an auditorium in memory of her husband, on property she had purchased on the north side of Dodge Street, directly west of Omaha's Central High School.[15] Many people later assumed that this indicated that including space for an art museum in the building was an afterthought on Sarah's part. In actuality, Sarah had been deeply committed to promoting the fine arts in Omaha for several decades and had been involved with previous efforts to establish an art museum in the city.

Before the opening of Sarah's Joslyn Memorial Art Museum in 1931, Omaha never had a true art museum. Art exhibits were held in churches, downtown buildings, and in Omaha hotels. The closest Omaha came to an actual museum were the semipermanent spaces provided through the efforts of George W. Lininger and Edith Tobitt. Lininger was a wealthy Omaha farm implements dealer and an art patron. He had amassed a large private collection of artwork. In 1888, he constructed an art gallery connected to his home to display his treasures. The gallery, open to the public on a limited basis, was operated under the auspices of the Western Art Association. The association disbanded and the gallery closed after his death in 1907. Miss Tobitt was the director of the Omaha Public Library from 1898 until 1934. She was active in promoting the fine arts in Omaha, and she often arranged to make space available for art exhibits at the library. Due to Miss Tobitt's efforts, the third floor of Omaha's main library was the city's de facto art museum for several years.

After the demise of the Western Art Association, the Omaha Fine Arts Society was formed. Several prominent Omaha women, including Sarah Joslyn, were founding members. A major goal of the group was the establishment of a permanent art museum in Omaha. The society began its first serious attempt to establish an art museum in 1914. In early March, the society formed a committee to raise funds to buy the Turner mansion, located at 3316 Farnam Street.[16] Sarah served on the committee in charge of publicity.

The society estimated that $50,000 would be necessary to purchase the structure and convert it into a museum. Their early fund-raising efforts appear to have been spectacularly successful. Within two weeks, they had raised over $30,000.[17] On May 12, 1914, Lula Belle Chase, head of the purchasing committee, abruptly announced that the group was abandoning the project, citing the committee's inability to raise the needed funds. She said that the society would return all donated funds.[18]

An *Omaha Excelsior* article later suggested that public criticism of the proposed location was the major reason for dropping the project. (Mrs. Chase's husband, Clement, published the *Excelsior*.) The article mentioned that the society had raised over $37,000 of the needed $50,000 before it ceased its efforts. It also noted that all the money had been returned.[19]

The committee had raised 75 percent of the needed funds in a little over a month and 60 percent in just three weeks. It seems odd that with this level of financial support, they were so easily persuaded to abandon their efforts. Other Omaha newspapers carried several stories about the museum. Their coverage was universally positive. In fact, there does not appear to have been any negative statements about the project in the press. Articles written about the project indicate that the effort had been very well planned. By early March 1914, several Omaha newspapers had printed detailed architectural drawings of the proposed museum.[20]

The *Excelsior* article hinted that besides the public's criticism of the proposed location for the museum, disagreements among committee members might have also played a part in the society's decision to abandon the project. This internal dissension may have been far more of a factor in the committee's decision than the undocumented public criticism. This may explain why Sarah later decided to bypass the Fine Arts Society and build her husband's memorial using only her own funds.

After this first attempt to establish a museum, nothing more was done until the end of World War I. In January 1919, the Fine Arts Society hosted an art exhibition at the new Fontenelle Hotel. John L. Webster, a local attorney and civic leader, wrote an editorial in which he complained about the poor attendance at the Fontenelle exhibit. He wrote that Omaha would never be a "first-class" city without a first-class art museum. He estimated that such a museum would cost $500,000 to build.[21]

After the war ended, David and Violet Magowan and their children returned to Omaha, and David returned to his job at the Western Newspaper Union. In early 1919, the Magowan family moved to New York City, where David would begin his new job with the company as vice president in charge of the advertising department. This left Sarah without her daughter or her grandchildren to occupy her life. After Violet and the twins left, Sarah began to concentrate on building the memorial to her husband.

In 1920, there were two more efforts to establish an art museum in the city. The first effort began in April. A bond issue for $250,000 was proposed to fund the construction of a new main public library in downtown Omaha.[22] The new structure would include a permanent art museum. This effort was doomed to failure from the start. Omaha already had built a large, expensive main library in 1894, and the facility was still in excellent shape.

Mrs. Ward Burgess, the president of the Omaha Fine Arts Society, spearheaded the second effort. She used her own money to hire a professional director for the society, who would serve for a three-year period. Although the director would be in charge of planning exhibits and lectures, the director's main duty would be to get a permanent museum built. In October, Maurice Block, formerly a curator at the Chicago Art Institute, was named the director of the Omaha Fine Arts Society.[23] Within days of his arrival, Block managed to antagonize the editors of the *Omaha Daily News*. In an editorial in the paper, they mildly rebuked Block for his comments that the Western states had been negligent of the fine arts. Block had suggested that the city would need to direct its efforts to correct this. The *Daily News* suggested that while it might be true that the West had been negligent in fostering the fine arts, it was because "it (the West) had been busily engaged in the 'arts' of home making, business, and agriculture," arts, the paper pointed out, "that were vastly more important."[24]

After this minor incident, Block settled into his job as director. His office was a desk on the second floor of Omaha's main library in a space provided by Edith Tobitt. He had an impressive record of achievements as director. He organized several well-received art exhibits. He also arranged a series of lectures featuring American artists and authors. His guest lecturers included Sinclair Lewis, Upton Sinclair, and Willa Cather. However, he was unsuccessful in his efforts to get a museum built. He served out his contract and left Omaha around 1925.

On the afternoon of Wednesday, December 27, 1922, Sarah held a press conference. She announced that she was going to spend $3 million to $5 million to construct an art museum in memory of her late husband. The museum would be located on the property she had purchased along Dodge Street. She announced that the firm of John and Alan McDonald would design the structure; they would also be in charge of its construction. She did not mention one small irony in the interview—that Mrs. Burgess's former home was one of the structures that would need to be torn down to make room for the new museum. The point was not lost on the reporters, however, and they included it in their stories the next day.[25]

The *Omaha Daily News* ran the most detailed account of the interview. The article noted that rumors about the impending construction of the museum had been rampant for more than a year, but that Sarah had refused to comment on her intentions. At one point in the interview, Sarah alluded to her penchant for secrecy, "You'd like to have me tell just how it will look when it's finished, wouldn't you? Well, I want to work out my plans before announcing them beforehand. It will come in its own good time, perhaps. Let's hope that there won't be another war which will turn everything topsy-turvy."[26]

In the interview, she discussed her motivations for building the memorial and the shape the structure would take. It was clear that her primary reason for building the memorial was to provide a home for the Fine Arts Society. It was also apparent that Sarah was still very much involved with the group. When asked why she was building the memorial, she replied, "I am doing this for my own pleasure. But, I do think the Omaha Society of Fine Arts deserves a home of its own. Each Sunday during the past month I have been acting as hostess at the art galleries in the city library; and I was surprised at the public interest in the exhibits."[27]

She continued to explain her motivations later in the interview:

But the Society of Fine Arts has been working under a handicap. Every time an exhibit comes in, our own pictures, which should be where the public can enjoy them all the time, have to be taken down and stowed away in some corner. In the building I am planning there will be plenty of room for both permanent and transient exhibits. The exhibits would also be more accessible. At the present time visitors to the art galleries must climb two flights of stairs.[28]

The size of the building was to be 186 by 436 feet. It would have three floors and an auditorium that would seat approximately two thousand people. The structure would incorporate an internal steel frame. The exterior would be clad in granite, the interior in marble. John and Alan McDonald said that they had been working on plans for the structure for over a year. They estimated the building would be completed within three years.[29] The civic and artistic communities were ecstatic over the announcement. The mayor and civic leaders would have all unanimously agreed with Edith Tobitt when she declared the idea of a memorial dedicated to the fine arts to be a "perfectly splendid one."[30]

Mrs. Burgess, still president of the Fine Arts Society, graciously commented on the proposed memorial:

> It's a wonderful gift. It will mean much for the city to have this sort of a building. And, of course it will make our work much more constructive, for we will know just what we have to do with, and what we are working towards, and how to accomplish our ends. It's the first really big thing which has ever been done towards the promotion of the arts in Omaha. And Omaha is about the only city that didn't have some such building. Mrs. Joslyn has done a marvelous thing.[31]

The McDonalds' estimate that the museum would be finished in three years was wildly off the mark. The building site sat idle for over five years. One of Sarah's obituaries alluded to one possible reason for this delay, noting that Sarah had spent the intervening time touring the country and looking at other museums to see how they were constructed and organized.[32] On the afternoon of Saturday, May 5, 1928, Sarah held another press conference with her architects. She unveiled detailed plans and drawings of the structure. She announced that work on the structure would begin immediately. One question not answered at the press conference was what she and her architects had been doing for the previous five years.

In addition to time spent studying other museums, several other possible reasons may explain the delay. First, neither Sarah nor George ever seemed to have been in a hurry to complete projects. Their estate of Lynhurst took over ten years to complete, and George's last project before his death, the Patterson Building, had been in progress for over a year when he announced plans for improving the property. A second reason is that John and Alan McDonald may have needed the extra time to design the complex structure. However, the main reason for the delay was probably a combination of issues regarding the control and financing of the memorial.

In 1928, just before her announcement, Sarah founded the Society of Liberal Arts. The group would oversee the construction and operation of the memorial. The society's founders included Sarah, Coit Farnsworth, Hubert H. Fish, John McDonald, Judge William A. Redick, and Charles W.

Russell. Farnsworth and Fish were WNU executives who worked for Sarah.[33] Judge Redick was a prominent Omaha lawyer who had been one of George Joslyn's closest friends; he was Sarah's personal attorney. Charles Russell was a wealthy Omaha businessman and a neighbor of Sarah's. John McDonald was her architect and friend.

The most revealing part of Sarah's announcement about the new group was that it would be headquartered at Lynhurst. The only logical reason for Sarah to form her own group, and not to simply donate the museum to the Art Institute of Omaha (the new name of the Omaha Society of Fine Arts), was that it allowed Sarah to have complete control of the memorial. Her creation of the society contradicts later accounts about the construction of the memorial that suggest that she did not play an active role in the project. Everyone on her board was someone she trusted, and a majority of its members were people who owed at least some of their livelihood to her.

Her desire to completely control the memorial and its construction may have been a result of her involvement with the Turner project in 1914. That effort had collapsed due to disagreements among the committee members; perhaps she did not want to repeat the incident. However, the most important reason for her desire to control the project was probably that the structure was to be a memorial to her husband. No devoted wife would leave that in the hands of others.

The second factor that may have delayed the construction of the memorial was a financial one. While Sarah was a very wealthy woman, she probably did not possess the resources to fund a five-million-dollar project without liquidating a substantial portion of her assets. On July 2, 1929, Sarah announced that she was selling her controlling interest in the Western Newspaper Union to a group of investors (led by Herbert H. Fish) for a reported $5,000,000.[34] She probably delayed taking this action until she needed the money to finance the construction of the memorial. It was almost certainly difficult for her to surrender control of the great empire her husband had built; however, once she made up her mind and solved her financial dilemma, work on the memorial proceeded swiftly.

Shortly after her Society of Liberal Arts was formed, its board appointed Dr. Paul Grummann as the first director of the museum. Dr. Grummann had been on the fine arts faculty at the University of Nebraska and was a popular lecturer with audiences in Lincoln and Omaha.[35] Dr. Grummann would become Sarah's closest confidant in the last few years of her life. She entrusted him with the memorial's direction and with the control of the bulk of her estate after her death. In 1940, the *Omaha World-Herald* published a letter Violet had written, in which she thanked Dr. Grummann for the work he had done on the memorial. Violet reminisced about a conversation she had with her mother shortly before Sarah died. Sarah had said to her, "I gave form to the Memorial and Professor Grummann gave it life."[36]

The Joslyn Memorial opened on Sunday, November 29, 1931. Crowds were lined up when the doors opened in the afternoon, and a steady stream of people toured the museum until it closed at 10:00 PM. The *Omaha World-Herald* estimated that over 25,000 people had visited the museum on its first day. The visitors on the first day were reported to have been amazed at the structure, with its marble walls and columns, and the huge fountain court with its beautifully tiled floor and exotic plantings. Sarah attended the memorial's opening day with a small group of her friends. They occupied chairs in one of the lower-level corridors. They sat there throughout most of the day, greeting friends and others who stopped by. Violet, who had come back from New York for the opening, spent the day with Sarah at the memorial.[37]

Late in the afternoon, Sarah and Violet attended the afternoon recital of Palmer Christian, a noted organist of the day, who gave a series of inaugural concerts in the new memorial's auditorium. They sat unobtrusively near the back of the hall to hear Mr. Christian perform on the auditorium's organ. The organ, which had been moved from Lynhurst to the memorial, was the same one that had so delighted George. Mr. Christian added a composition to his afternoon recital for Sarah and Violet. In the late afternoon, near the end of his performance, he played the "Largo" by Handel.[38]

Lynhurst's newly completed castle pictured in 1904, with its lower windows boarded up, and Jersey cows contentedly grazing in the foreground. George would continue his dispute with the State of Nebraska until 1906. Photograph attributed to the *Omaha Daily News*.

S. Archer Gibson seated at the controls of the Joslyns' Aeolian organ. This photograph appeared in the May 8, 1909 issue of the *Omaha Excelsior*.

The Joslyns' gardener, Isaac Roman, stands amid the ruins of the conservatory and greenhouse. Walter W. Scott took these photographs of the destruction at Lynhurst. He was one of the several professional photographers in Omaha who spent the day after the tornado struck wandering through the city and photographing the devastation. Several of Mr. Scott's photographs later appeared as postcards and in *The Track of the Tornado*, published by the Omaha Bee Company in 1913.

Mr. Roman surveys the interior of the devastated palm house. Photograph from the Douglas County Historical Society (Archive Collections).

The intrepid Mr. Roman climbed atop the music room roof to assess the extensive damage the tornado did to the Joslyns' castle. Photograph from the Nebraska State Historical Society (Photographic Collection).

The Joslyns' daughter, Violet, and her twin daughters, seated on the chair swing that once hung on the mansion's front porch. Photograph courtesy of the Friends of Joslyn Castle.

George sits in contemplation on the same swing, shortly before his death in 1916. Photograph courtesy of the Friends of Joslyn Castle.

Sarah proudly stands in front of a Stevens-Duryea touring car in this 1925 Louis Bostwick photograph. The arched entrance of Lynhurst Castle's porte cochere is visible in the background. Photograph from the Bostwick-Frohardt collection of the Durham Western Heritage Museum.

Sarah's beautiful pink marble memorial to George, as it appears today. Photograph by author.

10

Sarah's Legacy (1932–1940)

The Extortion Plot

When the Joslyn Memorial opened, Sarah was nearly eighty years old. She had created a magnificent structure, but it had cost her over three million dollars. The building of the memorial had been fraught with minor setbacks. Sarah was frequently frustrated with the slow pace of construction and some costly redesigns. She had reason to be concerned. While she was still a very wealthy woman, the construction of the Joslyn Memorial had probably consumed over half of her fortune. It was the crowning achievement of her life, but it had been expensive.

Once the construction process was over, Sarah divided her time between Lynhurst and the memorial. When at the memorial, she would often visit the reception room. It is a large room with elegant wood paneling and a beautiful marble fireplace located on the first floor at the west side of the structure. Occasionally, she would sit in the room alone in contemplation. In the late afternoon, the long, narrow stained-glass windows set in the western wall, decorated with cascading ivy leaves on a cobalt blue background, would blaze a brilliant blue and green when lit by the setting sun. The falling leaves of ivy, an ancient symbol of devotion, may have comforted her as she thought about her departed husband.

During this period, she began to receive a series of letters from people pleading for her help. The period of the construction and early years of the memorial coincided with the Great Depression, one of the worst economic disasters ever to befall the United States. At its height in 1933, over one-fourth of the population was unemployed. Many people affected by the Depression were forced to beg for assistance from anyone whom they thought might be able to aid them. Sarah was the recipient of hundreds of letters begging her for money. Some individuals who wrote her went beyond merely asking her for relief and threatened her if she did not come to their aid.

In their 1991 interview, Sarah's granddaughters recalled being present when she opened one of these letters. Sarah had been sitting at her desk in the morning room, reading her mail, when the twins entered the room. They said they saw Sarah sitting silently with a look of horror on her face. An opened letter was lying on the floor beside her. They said that their mother later told them Sarah had received another threatening letter. The twins indicated that this was a common occurrence.[1]

The best-documented of these threats was an extortion attempt that began on the morning of Saturday, April 14, 1934, when Sarah received an anonymous letter in the mail. The letter's author demanded an undisclosed sum of money and threatened to damage the memorial if Sarah failed to meet the letter-writer's demands. Sarah had good reason to take this threat seriously. Only a few months before, unknown vandals had splashed black paint on the marble steps of the structure. The letter implied that a similar act of vandalism would occur if she did not comply.[2]

She immediately called the authorities, and the letter was turned over to postal inspectors. A large task force composed of Omaha police and postal inspectors was formed to investigate the threat. Following directions in the letter, on Monday, April 16, the inspectors placed an ad in the local newspaper. It read simply: "Sam. Will comply. Furnish details. J."[3]

On Tuesday, a second letter arrived. The writer instructed Sarah to prepare a package containing $1,000 wrapped in newspaper. The second letter also stated that further instructions would be sent in a final letter. On Friday, the third letter arrived. It instructed her that someone would arrive on Saturday evening to pick up the package. This letter may have also contained a code phrase the person would use. On Saturday evening, a young man rang the mansion's doorbell and announced to the maid who answered the door, "I have come for the package for Sam."[4]

She quietly handed him the package, and he turned and left. As the young man walked to the front gate, he was unaware that two postal inspectors inside the house had witnessed the exchange. He also did not see the seven Omaha police detectives, hidden in positions on the Joslyn grounds, who were intently watching him. He walked one block south and boarded a streetcar bound for downtown Omaha. Omaha Police Captain Fritz Frank followed the young man onto the car and sat in the seat directly in front of him. Detective Inspector Anderson, who was also following the suspect, sat directly behind the young man. In addition to the two officers, three police cars unobtrusively escorted the streetcar as it slowly headed east.

Soon two more young men boarded the streetcar. One sat next to the young suspect, and the other stood near the front of the car. At the next stop, the young man standing at the front of the car got off, while the other young man continued to sit with the suspect. A few moments later, the second young man left the streetcar with the package wrapped in newspaper while the would-be extortionist remained seated. The officers arrested the second young man as he dismounted the car. It later turned out that this young man had nothing to do with the plot; he had merely been a friend of the suspect's and had sat with him to say hello.

Unbeknownst to the investigators, the young man who had been standing at the front of the car was the second extortionist. He had panicked and fled when he saw someone sitting with his accomplice. By Sunday, the incident was over. Omer Fleming, the innocent young man, had been cleared and released. The police had arrested the man who had picked up the package at Lynhurst when he attempted to leave the streetcar at the next stop. He was identified as seventeen-year-old John E. Flanagan, a Creighton University freshman from New York. He was the nephew of Father Edward Flanagan, the founder of Boys Town, and had been sent to Omaha in the hope that his uncle could watch over him. Young Flanagan quickly confessed his role in the plot. He revealed that his partner was eighteen-year-old Edward Muffitt, also a freshman at the university. Muffitt, the son of an insurance executive, was an Omaha native. When he was arrested at his parents' home, he told the arresting officers, "We started this as a joke and kept getting further and further into it. We didn't know when to stop."[5]

Stories detailing the plot appeared in several major newspapers. The two young men were charged under the new "Lindbergh Law," a law that had recently been passed by the United States Congress in response to the kidnapping and murder of the infant son of Charles Lindbergh. The law made kidnapping and extortion federal crimes and imposed penalties of up to $1,000 in fines and twenty years in prison.[6]

Reporters interviewed Sarah on Sunday morning after the young men had been arrested. She was torn between her commitment to the welfare of young people and her outrage over the crime. When asked about what she felt the young criminals' fate should be, she replied, "It's a terrible thing; I can't help feeling sorry for the boys when I think of what this might mean to them. I feel more sorry however for their parents. The matter is out of my hands however. I'll leave their punishment to the courts."[7]

Sarah's Legacy

The extortion attempt had been a traumatic experience for Sarah. After it ended, she returned to her quiet life of attending church and occasionally visiting the memorial. She entertained only a small circle of close friends at her home. She stayed active in the charitable causes she supported. Increasingly, however, she would ask the people involved to come to her home to meet with her. Only a week before she died, she met for over two hours in her home with Gould Dietz, president of the Nebraska Humane Society. Dietz was the son of Sarah's friend Leonora Dietz; he later said that he had first become involved with the organization at Sarah's request.[8]

Sarah made rare public appearances during the last few years of her life. In 1937, she attended an event honoring her for her donation of an Aeolian-Skinner organ to the First Unitarian Church, the church she had attended since 1893.[9] The same year, she received one of the first honorary doctorates awarded by Omaha University, in a ceremony on its campus. She was awarded the degree in recognition of the contributions George had made to the university and of her continued financial support of the institution.[10]

In the last year of her life, her health began to fail. As she became more ill, she receded almost completely from public view and almost never left Lynhurst. In the fall of 1939, her condition deteriorated, and by late October, she was confined to her bed. During this time, she would call out to her cook, Hannah Flicker, as Hannah passed her door, saying, "Hannah, I'm still here."[11]

In early 1940, Sarah seemed to rally. She began to resume a limited schedule of activities. She even resumed her earlier passion for going on daily automobile rides with her chauffeur. In mid-February, Sarah's condition worsened, and she was again bedridden. Her doctors diagnosed her as suffering from pneumonia and pleurisy. At first, they did not consider her condition to be life-threatening. At 6:15 on the morning of Wednesday, February 28, 1940, she asked her nurse for some water; moments later, she was dead.

The *Omaha World-Herald* carried her obituary on its front page. It listed the many acts of charity she and her husband had performed. It noted that she had given $4,600,000 to the Joslyn Memorial during her life. Funeral services for Sarah Joslyn were held on Saturday afternoon, March 2, 1940, at 2:30 PM.[12] David, Violet, their children, her niece Angie, and a few of Sarah's closest friends attended the small private service held for her at Lynhurst. There were no reporters present.

On March 5, 1940, the *World-Herald* published the details of her will, along with photographs of the interior of the castle. She had left an estate valued at $3.2 million. Along with the amounts she left to Violet and other family members, she left large sums to several charities in Omaha.

Sarah's charitable bequests reflected her interests. She left $50,000 to both Omaha University and the First Unitarian Church. She also forgave a $50,000 debt the Nebraska Humane Society owed her. Sarah left $5,000 to the Piney Woods School in Braxton, Mississippi, a school for African American children. She also left $5,000 each to Social Settlement of Omaha, the Hattie B. Monroe Home for Crippled Children, the Visiting Nurse Association, and the Fontenelle Boulevard Home (the new name of the Old People's Home). She left $3,000 each to the Omaha Women's Club, the Friends of Music, the Omaha YWCA, the Salvation Army, the Child Savings Institute, and the Joseph Joslin Memorial Library in Waitsfield. She also gave the library many of her books.[13]

Everything else, including the Lynhurst estate, went to the Society for Liberal Arts, the organization she had founded to operate the memorial. After subtracting the specific bequests she had made, this left the society with over $2.5 million. With this final bequest, the total amount she gave to the memorial was over $7 million .[14]

She left little behind of a personal nature. Unlike her husband, no grand monument honors her. Sarah was interred with her husband in a simple, yet elegant mausoleum set on a hill north of the city. On it is carved only the name Joslyn, and nothing more. Its only adornment is a small, beautiful stained-glass window depicting a tranquil pond.

By all measures, Sarah had lived a good life. She had lived in a beautiful home, traveled as she wished, attended lavish parties, and cultivated a fabulous orchid collection. She had wanted for nothing, and yet Sarah had been a modest woman. Even before her husband died, she had maintained a low profile; yet, while perhaps shy, she worked tirelessly to benefit her community.

Sarah helped promote a variety of educational and charitable causes. She donated not just her money, but also her time and labor. She was a wealthy woman who swept the floors of the Old People's Home herself.[15] She was an elderly widow who opened her heart and the doors of her home to hundreds of young soldiers she did not know.

Perhaps the best eulogy for Sarah Joslyn was written long before her death. In early November 1907, as winter set in, Sarah gave John C. Gordon $300. Gordon was an invalid who eked out a subsistence living selling magazine subscriptions. In a brief comment on Sarah's donation, the *Omaha Excelsior* noted that "others will doubtless remember the kind deed longer than Mrs. Joslyn, who is doing so much good in the world in her own unostentatious way."[16]

While it may seem that the reputations of George and Sarah Joslyn have fared poorly, they have done much better than most of their contemporaries. The families who built Omaha are largely forgotten today. The mention of the names of most of Omaha's original first families will invite a blank stare. The names Bidwell, Dietz, Wattles, Yost, Yates, and even those of the Kountze brothers mean little to most Omaha residents. Today they are remembered only through the churches or schools they funded. The public does not remember their very real contributions to the growth and prosperity of Omaha, the State of Nebraska, and the nation.

Perhaps Sarah Joslyn knew best, for she created a memorial in name only. While static remembrances of her adored husband cover the outside of the building, the inside houses an ever-changing display of vibrant artwork. Its auditorium hosts musicians and lecturers of every kind. People who enter the memorial are not somber or reflective; they are inquisitive and excited about what they might see or hear. The outside of the Joslyn Memorial might be a memorial to George's memory, but what goes on inside is a living tribute to Sarah.

Epilogue (1940–2006)

After Sarah's funeral, the Magowans returned to their home in Scarsdale, New York. David continued to work for the Western Newspaper Union until his death at age sixty-five on April 16, 1952.[1] Violet survived him for thirty years until her death in March 1983, at the age of ninety.[2] The couple had adopted a young man named David, who died in 1999.[3] Sally Magowan married John Hersey in 1946.[4] She died in 1997 at the age of eighty-three.[5] Joslyn Magowan married Luther Birdzell in 1943.[6] She died on December 7, 2005, at the age of ninety-one.[7] Coit Farnsworth died in 1937. The last mention of Angie Farnsworth was in Sarah's obituary in 1940, when Angie was seventy-one years old. In an interview conducted on August 9, 1944, Anne Traub (Sarah's personal secretary) indicated that Angie had remarried and moved to Chicago.[8]

The last mention of George Bidwell is a visit he and his wife made to Sarah in December 1918, when he was seventy-one years old.[9] His wife, Hattie, lived until 1935. She, and presumably Mr. Bidwell, are buried in the Hollywood Forever Cemetery in Los Angeles, California.[10] Judge William Redick continued to serve on the board of the Society of Liberal Arts until his death in May 1936.[11] Sarah's friends Lula Belle and Clement Chase ran into financial difficulties in 1921 and moved to Chicago to live near their daughter, Carmelita Hinton. An accomplished artist, Lula Belle continued painting and exhibiting her work until she died in Orlando on February 6, 1950, at eighty-four.[12] Archer Gibson continued to serve as house organist for wealthy families for several years. He also began performing on the radio and made numerous recordings for RCA. He died on July 15, 1952, at the age of seventy-six.[13]

Charles G. Carpenter continued to work as a landscape architect. After he completed his work at Lynhurst, he worked for two years as an engineer for the Omaha Board of Parks. In 1905, he appears to have left Omaha.[14] John Thorpe continued his career as a floriculturist until his death in 1909. In 1964, the Society of American Florists inducted him into their hall of fame.[15] John and Alan McDonald continued their practice in Omaha until Alan died at age fifty-six in 1947. He is interred in the chapel of Omaha's Forest Lawn Cemetery, a building designed by his father in 1911.[16] John McDonald continued working until just before his death in 1956; he was ninety-five years old. Like Judge Redick, he served on the board of the Society of Liberal Arts until his death.[17]

After Sarah's death, Lynhurst stood empty for three years, while the Society of Liberal Arts debated what to do with the estate. Finally, they offered it to the Omaha Public Schools (OPS) for use as its headquarters. OPS used the estate from 1944 until 1989, when the school system decided the estate buildings no longer met their needs. In 1989, the headquarters of the school system moved to Omaha's Technical High School. After the move, OPS attempted to sell the estate. When no buyers appeared, Omaha's Landmarks Incorporated enlisted the aid of state senator Brad Ashford and convinced the State of Nebraska to take control of the structure.

Today, the Joslyns' estate remains controlled by the state. The Joslyn Castle Institute manages the estate. The University of Nebraska's College of Architecture formed the institute to foster sustainable community development. A second mission of the organization is to preserve and restore Lynhurst. A second group that is helping to preserve and restore the estate is the Friends of Joslyn Castle. Since 1990, the Friends have raised thousands of dollars to this end. In 2003, the Friends were able to restore Sarah's morning room to its original condition. In 2005, they restored Joslyn Castle's drawing room light fixtures and ceiling. Currently the group is repairing and restoring the castle's exterior windows.

Sarah's memorial to her husband remains a vibrant cultural institution in the city. In the late 1980s, the museum board began planning for much-needed renovation and expansion of the facility. These efforts culminated on November 19, 1994, when it opened a new thirty-thousand-square-foot wing to the public.[18] Connected to the original structure by a glass atrium, the addition is faced with the same marble as the memorial. It provides a large, modern display space that makes extensive use of natural light.

When the memorial was opened more than sixty years earlier, William F. Baxter, a prominent Omaha businessman, was selected to accept Sarah's gift to the city. During the dedication ceremonies, he praised Sarah's thoughtfulness in providing a memorial museum that would benefit Omaha. "It is generous, it is thoughtful. It is magnificent. It stands and will stand for generations as a monitor, as a stimulant, as an inspiration to all the finer things of human life."[19] Baxter's insights are as appropriate today as they were in 1931.

Chapter Notes

Introduction:

1. *Omaha World-Herald*, October 5, 1916: 4.

2. *Omaha Daily Bee*, August 26, 1897: 3; Connie Adams-Pitt; *The 1889 Cincinnati Bell Telephone Book*, Book E (2001). http://www.rootsweb.com/~kycchgs/BOOK_E.htm (March 26, 2005).

Page three of the *Omaha Daily Bee* features one of thousands of "Big G" display advertisements that appeared in newspapers around the country. All of the advertisements clearly identified the purveyor of "Big G" as the Evans Chemical Company, located in Cincinnati, Ohio. On the same page, there is also an advertisement for Cook Remedy's elixir.

The *1889 Cincinnati Telephone Directory* has this listing for the company: Evans Chemical Co., A.H. Evans Pres't, 49 West Pearl St.

Chapter One:

1. Transcript, Sally Hersey and Joslyn Birdzell Oral History Interview, September 26, 1991, by Audrey Kauders, Elizabeth Garrison, Ruby Hagerbaumer, and Lannie McNichols (Archives of the Joslyn Castle Institute for Sustainable Communities).

2. Church of Jesus Christ of Latter-Day Saints (LDS) family search: Joseph Joslin; spouse: Nancy; date: 1800 (2005). http://www.familysearch.org/Eng/Search/frameset_search.asp (April 19, 2005).

The Church of the Latter-Day Saints maintains one of the largest and most sophisticated genealogical libraries in the United States. They also have an efficient online search engine that was used extensively in researching the Joslyns, their family, and their friends for this work. Each entry notes the search terms that will lead to the results quoted. This book would not have been possible without their gracious cooperation.

3. *Omaha World-Herald*, February 28, 1940: 1, 6.

4. LDS search: Joseph Joslin; spouse: Abigail Taylor; date: 1817 (April 19, 2005).

5. LDS search: George Joslin; father: Alfred Joslin; date: 1848 (August 3, 2005).

6. Diantha Howard and Maggie Seward; 1850 Census of Washington County, Vermont. http://www.rootsweb.com/~vtwashin/Census/CENSINDX.HTM (August 1, 2005).

7. Central Vermont Chamber of Commerce; History of Town of Waitsfield, Vermont (2003). http://www.central-vt.com/towns/history/HstWait.htm (April 19, 2005).

8. Jalanne C. Barnes; Waitsfield Township, Washington County. http://freepages.genealogy.rootsweb.com/~vermontgenealogyresources/Townships/Washington/Waitsfield-town.html (March 23, 2005).

9. *Omaha Daily News*, October 4, 1916: 1, 3.

10. Dennis Mihelich, "George Joslyn: America's First Media Mogul," *Nebraska History* (Spring 2001): 26–37.

11. Tara Maginnis, "The Costumer's Manifesto" http://www.costumes.org/history/100pages/collarsmen.htm (August 3, 2005).

12. Graham W. J. Beale, *Joslyn Art Museum: A Building History*, Joslyn Art Museum (1994): 7.

13. *Omaha World-Herald*, February 28, 1940: 1, 6.

14. Dennis Mihelich, "The Joslyns of Omaha: Opulence and Philanthropy," *Nebraska History* (Spring 2002): 2–14.

15. Linda Suarez, *History of Polk County, Iowa* (Des Moines: Union Publishing Company, 1880): 763. http://www.rootsweb.com/~iabiog/polk/h1880/h1880.htm (March 30, 2005).

16. *Des Moines City Directory* (1870–1880); *1880–81 Omaha City Directory.*

17. Suarez, *History of Polk County.*

18. Elmo Scott Watson, *A History of Newspaper Syndicates in the United States* (Chicago, 1936): 1–2.

19. Ibid., 3–4.

20. Ibid., 22.

21. Ibid., 36.

22. *New York Times*, February 8, 1952: 30.

23. *New York Times*, April 3, 1961: 44.

24. International Paper Company, "Timeline." http://www.internationalpaper.com/Our%20 Company/About%20Us/Paper%20Making%20Timeline.html (November 21, 2005).

25. Watson, *History of Newspaper Syndicates*: 31.

26. *Omaha Excelsior*, January 4, 1890: 1.

27. Watson, *History of Newspaper Syndicates*: 53–54.

28. Watson, *History of Newspaper Syndicates*: 39; *New York Times*, August 4, 1912: 8.

Chapter Two:

1. *Omaha Daily Bee*, September 19, 1910: 1.

2. *1886 Omaha City Directory* (OCD).

3. OCD, 1885: 479.

4. *Omaha Daily Bee*, October 28, 1882: 2.

5. *Omaha Excelsior*, January 4, 1890: 1.

6. OCD, 1886.

7. *Omaha Excelsior*, July 26, 1890: 1.

8. LDS search: Ferdinand Joslin (April 8. 2005).

9. OCD, 1882–83.

10. LDS search: Rose Starkey (April 9, 2005).

11. Omaha Public Library, Douglas County Marriage Records (DCMR): Joslin, Ferdinand.

12. OCD, 1884, 1885.

13. Transcript, Sally Hersey and Joslyn Birdzell Oral History Interview, September 26, 1991, by Audrey Kauders, Elizabeth Garrison, Ruby Hagerbaumer, and Lannie McNichols (Archives of the Joslyn Castle Institute for Sustainable Communities).

14. OCD, 1889 through 1918.

15. LDS search: Ferdinand Joslin (April 9, 2005).

16. Forest Lawn Cemetery Association (FLCA), Last Name Lookup: J. http://www.forestlawnomaha.com/GraveIndex/IndexSummaryJ.html (April 9, 2005).

It should be noted that Forest Lawn's Web site does not identify where Ferdinand is buried and it is my assumption that he is buried near Mary. And, of course, their Web site spells his name Fred.

17. LDS search: Frederick Joslin; spouse: Ina; date: 1883 (April 9, 2005).

18. OCD, 1885 through 1894.

19. *Omaha World-Herald*, October 9, 1916: 1–2.

20. LDS search: George Joslin; date: 1848 (April 9, 2005).

21. LDS search: Jennie Joslin; date: 1880 (April 9, 2005).

This analysis was conducted using the "next household" search feature of the LDS site. This allowed for a house-by-house search of the households near Jennie's residence in the 1880 census.

22. OCD, 1885 through 1889.

23. DCMR: Joslin, Jennie.

24. FLCA: S. http://www.forestlawnomaha.com/GraveIndex/IndexSummaryS.html (April 9, 2005); Jessie Brain Tombstone, Forest Lawn Cemetery. Section MAS-733-6; OCD, 1908.

25. DCMR: Spence, Jessie.

26. OCD, 1908 through 1915.

27. Sarah Joslyn's will (Archives of the Joslyn Castle Institute for Sustainable Communities).

28. FCLA: M. http://www.forestlawnomaha.com/GraveIndex/IndexSummaryM.html (April 9, 2005).

29. LDS search: Lucelia Selleck; date: 1837 (April 9, 2005).

30. LDS search: Eugene Boyce; spouse: Lucilia; date: 1843 (April 9, 2005).

31. LDS search: Eugene Boyce (April 10, 2005).

32. LDS search: Lucilia Sophia Selleck (April 19, 2005).

33. LDS search: Eugene Boyce (April 10, 2005).

34. OCD, 1888 through 1892.

35. *Omaha Excelsior*, February 2, 1889: 5.

36. *World-Herald*, 1–2.

37. *Omaha Excelsior*, March 24, 1917: 13.

38. FLCA: F. http://www.forestlawnomaha.com/GraveIndex/IndexSummaryF.html (April 10, 2005).

39. LDS search: John McDonald; date: 1861 (April 10, 2005).

40. OCD, 1886 through 1893.

41. City of Omaha, Planning Department Archives.

This assumption of McDonald's involvement is based on his name appearing on the first building permits taken out for structures on the Joslyns' estate in 1897.

42. *Omaha World-Herald*, October 5, 1916: 4.

43. LDS search: Oliver Campbell; date: 1833 (April 10, 2005).

44. OCD, 1870 through 1914.

45. 1900 United States Census: Douglas County, Nebraska.

46. Nebraska Game and Parks Commission, "Cowboy Trail." http://www.ngpc.state.ne.us/parks/guides/trails/cowboy/cowboy.asp (March 23, 2005).

47. *Nebraskans: 1854-1904* (Omaha Bee Publishing, 1904): 11.

48. *Omaha World-Herald*, August 28, 1909: 6.

49. *Omaha Excelsior*, August 24, 1912: 13.

Chapter Three:

1. Laura Elmendorf-Skeels, "The Joscelyn-Joslin Family," *Journal of American History* 6 (1912): 517–526.

2. Lyndhurst, a National Trust Historic Site, "A Short History of Lyndhurst" (2002). http://www.lyndhurst.org/history.html (March 23, 2005).

3. *Omaha Excelsior*, April 8, 1893: 6.

4. *Omaha World-Herald*, April 6, 1910: 9.

5. Ibid.

6. *Omaha Daily News*, July 14, 1909: 1.

7. *World-Herald*, 9.

8. *Omaha Daily News*, March 23, 1924: 3C.

9. *Omaha Excelsior*, June 17, 1893: 6.

10. *Omaha Excelsior*, September 23, 1893: 6.

11. eCUIP: The Digital Library, "Chicago: City of Neighborhoods," Chicago South Lakefront Tour: Site M. http://ecuip.lib.uchicago.edu/diglib/social/cityofneighborhoods/southlakefront/con_tour_m.html (July 28, 2004).

12. Kristin Standaert, "World's Columbian Exposition of 1893" (Paul V. Galvin Library Collection, Illinois Institute of Technology): *The Book of the Fair* (1999): 956–960. http://columbus.gl.iit.edu/bookfair/bftoc.html (March 23, 2005).

13. *New York Times*, August 22, 1891: 5.

14. *New York Times*, December 19, 1891: 5.

15. *New York Times*, May 24, 1893: 2.

16. Kristin Standaert, "World's Columbian Exposition of 1893" (Paul V. Galvin Library Collection, Illinois Institute of Technology): *The Dream City* (1998). http://columbus.gl.iit.edu/dreamcity/00024043.html (March 23, 2005).

17. Robert E. Grese, *Jens Jensen: Maker of Natural Parks and Gardens* (Johns Hopkins University Press, 1992): 62–63.

18. *Omaha World-Herald*, August 29, 1897: 12.

19. *Omaha Excelsior*, February 23, 1893: 6; *Excelsior*, April 1, 1893: 7.

20. *Omaha Excelsior*, February 18, 1893: 6.

21. City of Omaha, Planning Department Archives.

22. *Omaha Excelsior*, August 28, 1897: 7.

23. *World-Herald*, 12.

24. *Omaha World-Herald*, August 27, 1944: 10A.

25. Cor Kwant, "Ginkgo Biloba: The Ginkgo Pages" (2005). http://www.xs4all.nl/~kwanten/thetree.htm (August 3, 2005).

26. *Omaha Excelsior*, August 28, 1897: 7.

27. Ibid.

The admission receipts totaled $300. Admission for adults was twenty-five cents and admission for children was ten cents. Three hundred dollars would equal the admission of 1,200 adults, or 3,000 children. Several people also worked as volunteers at the event.

28. Ibid.

29. *New York Times*, November 16, 1894: 2.

30. *Omaha Excelsior*, September 7, 1918: 2.

The *Excelsior* article does not list the types of tricks the animals performed. The ones I have listed are common tricks taught to performing horses.

Chapter Four:

1. *Omaha Excelsior*, September 18, 1897: 6.

2. *Omaha Daily News*, October 12, 1913: 5C; Digital Photographs (Archives of the Joslyn Castle Institute for Sustainable Communities).

The sizes of the various structures listed were estimated by using a published report in the *Omaha Daily News*, analysis of archival photographs, and by measuring the remaining foundation of the greenhouse.

3. Ibid.

4. Susan Orlean, *The Orchid Thief* (Random House, 1998): 64–65.

5. *New York Times*, August 31, 1897: 7; *Times*, June 22, 1902: 27.

6. *Times*, June 22, 1902: 27.

7. Ibid.

8. *New York Times*, September 26, 1907: 1.

9. Palm & Cycad Societies of Australia, "John Gould Veitch 1839–1870," http://www.pacsoa.org.au/places/People/veitch.html (August 3, 2005); *Orchid Thief*, 57.

10. *Times*, June 22, 1902.

11. *New York Times*, March 17, 1889: 4.

12. Ibid.

13. Orlean, *Orchid Thief*, 58–59.

14. *Omaha Daily Bee*, March 26, 1913: 9; *Omaha Daily News*, April 17, 1913: 3.

15. *Omaha Daily News*, March 29, 1913: 3.

16. Ibid.

17. *Excelsior*, 6.

18. *New York Times*, February 25, 1887: 8.

19. City of Omaha, Planning Department Archives.

20. *Omaha Excelsior*, July 2, 1898: 1–2.

21. *Omaha Excelsior*, August 13, 1898: 2-3; *Excelsior*, September 24, 1898: 3.

22. *Omaha Excelsior*, October 15, 1898: 1.

23. Ibid.

While it is entirely possible that George and Sarah met a U.S. president prior to this event, I was unable to find any account of such a meeting.

24. LDS search: Violet Magowan (November 26, 2005).

25. Laws of Nebraska, Nebraska Statutes and Constitution; searchable statutes, Constitution, UCC and Appendices database, Section 43-101.2004, http://statutes.unicam.state.ne.us/Corpus/statutes/chap43/R4301001.html (March 24, 2005).

26. *Omaha Excelsior*, June 4, 1910: 12.

27. *Omaha Excelsior*, May 4, 1901: 1.

28. Ibid.

29. *Omaha World-Herald* (Section Two), May 5, 1901: 12.

30. *Excelsior*, 12.

31. City of Omaha, Planning Department Archives.

32. *Omaha Excelsior*, June 21, 1902: 3.

33. *Omaha Daily News*, November 14, 1903: 5.

34. *Omaha Excelsior*, June 21, 1902: 3.

35. *Omaha Daily News*, November 14, 1903: 1.

36. Effie Athanassapouls et al., *Joslyn Castle Estate: Cultural Landscape Report.* (Omaha, Landmarks, Inc., 1997): 18.

37. The Royal Commission on the Ancient and Historical Monuments of Scotland, "Scottish Baronial Splendor at Threave House" (2004), http://www.rcahms.gov.uk/highlightthreave.html (March 24, 2005).

38. Cyril M. Harris, ed., *Dictionary of Architecture & Construction* (Third edition, 2000).

39. *Omaha Excelsior*, May 4, 1901: 1.

Chapter Five:

1. *1895 City of Chicago Telephone Directory.*

2. Effie Athanassapouls et al., *Joslyn Castle Estate: Cultural Landscape Report* (Omaha, Landmarks, Inc., 1997): 18.

3. City of Omaha, Planning Department Archives.

4. Rollin Smith, *The Aeolian Pipe Organ and Its Music* (Smith, 1998): 331–32.

5. Morgan S. Friedman, "The Inflation Calculator" (2003), http://www.westegg.com/inflation/ (March 24, 2005).

6. Smith, *The Aeolian Pipe Organ*, 165.

7. Allison Ledes Eckardt, "Frank Lloyd Wright's collaborator—Works by Wright and George Mann Niedecken will be exhibited in a series of shows," *Magazine Antiques* (1999), http://www.findarticles.com/p/articles/mi_m1026/is_3_155/ai_54169320#continue (July 30, 2005).

8. Quezal Art Glass Reference Information, "History @ Collectics," Antiques & Collectibles, http://www.collectics.com/education_quezal.html (March 24, 2005).

9. *Omaha Excelsior*, October 29, 1892: 1.

10. *Omaha Excelsior*, June 10, 1893: 7.

11. *Omaha Excelsior*, December 24, 1904: 13.

Chapter Six:

1. Pam Rietsch, Carrole Miller, and Ted Miller, "Nebraska Legislature 1903–4" (2002): 26, 64, http://www.rootsweb.com/~neresour/OLLibrary/Legislature/1903/(March 24, 2005).

2. *Omaha Daily News*, January 5, 1903: 1–2.

3. *Omaha World-Herald*, March 8, 1903: 1.

4. *Omaha World-Herald*, March 4, 1903: 1.

5. *Omaha World-Herald*, April 9, 1903: 1.

6. *Omaha World-Herald*, March 10, 1903: 1–2.

7. *Omaha Daily News*, October 24, 1903: 1.

8. *Omaha Daily News*, April 30, 1904: 1.

9. Ibid.

10. *Omaha Daily News*, May 20, 1904: 1.

11. *Omaha World-Herald*, March 6, 1903: 1.

12. *Omaha Daily News*, June 6, 1904: 1.

13. *Omaha Excelsior*, July 16, 1904: 2–3.

14. *New York Times*, June 26, 1904: 14.

15. *Excelsior,* 2.

16. *Omaha World-Herald*, June 6, 1904: 1.

17. *Excelsior,* 2.

18. *Omaha Excelsior*, July 7, 1906: 3.

19. Laws of Nebraska, Nebraska Statutes and Constitution: searchable statutes, Constitution, UCC and Appendices database, Section 77-201, Annotation One (2004), http://statutes. unicam.state.ne.us/Corpus/statutes/chap77/R7702001.html (August 4, 2005).

20. Laws of Nebraska, Nebraska Statutes and Constitution: searchable statutes, Constitution, UCC and Appendices database, Section 77-601, Annotation Three (2004), http://statutes. unicam.state.ne.us/Corpus/statutes/chap77/R7702001.html (August 4, 2005).

21. Laws of Nebraska, Nebraska Statutes and Constitution: searchable statutes, Constitution, UCC and Appendices database, Section CVIII-1, Annotation Eight (2004), http://statutes. unicam.state.ne.us/Corpus/chapC/CVIII-1.html (August 4, 2005).

22. Laws of Nebraska, Nebraska Statutes and Constitution: searchable statutes, Constitution, UCC and Appendices database, Section 77-202, Item Seven (2004), http://statutes. unicam.state.ne.us/Corpus/statutes/chap77/R7702002.html (August 4, 2005).

Chapter Seven:

1. *Omaha Excelsior*, January 11, 1908: 10.

2. *Omaha Excelsior*, November 14, 1908: 12.

3. Rollin Smith, *The Aeolian Pipe Organ and Its Music* (Smith, 1998): 244–256.

4. *New York Times*, June 7, 1909: 7.

5. Smith, *The Aeolian Pipe Organ.*

6. Smith, *The Aeolian Pipe Organ.*

7. Smith, *The Aeolian Pipe Organ.*

8. *Omaha Excelsior*, June 5, 1909: 6.

9. *Omaha Excelsior*, May 3, 1913: 3.

10. *Excelsior,* 12.

11. *Times*, 7.

12. *Omaha Excelsior*, October 31, 1914: 11.

13. *New York Times*, February 3, 1909: 1.

14. Shibusawa Ei'ichi Memorial Foundation (2004), http://www.shibusawa.or.jp/english/index.html (March 25, 2005).

15. David Henderson and Greg Dobbs, Boomer Café, "Cherry Blossoms" (2003), http://www.boomercafe.com/blossoms/cherryblossoms.htm (March 25, 2005).

16. *Washington Post*, September 2, 1909: 7.

17. *New York Times*, November 29, 1909: 15.

18. *Omaha Daily News*, November 14, 1909: 1–2.

19. Ibid.

20. Ibid.

21. *Omaha Excelsior*, November 20, 1909: 1–2.

22. Ibid.

23. *Omaha Excelsior*, May 14, 1910: 3.

24. *Omaha Excelsior*, December 16, 1905: 14.

25. *Omaha Excelsior*, September 18, 1909: 11.

26. *Omaha Excelsior*, September 15, 1917: 12.

27. *Omaha Excelsior*, August 17, 1912: 11.

28. Transcript, Sally Hersey and Joslyn Birdzell Oral History Interview, September 26, 1991, by Audrey Kauders, Elizabeth Garrison, Ruby Hagerbaumer, and Lannie McNichols (Archives of the Joslyn Castle Institute for Sustainable Communities).

29. *Omaha Excelsior*, March 15, 1913: 11.

Chapter Eight:

1. *Omaha Daily News* (magazine section), March 30, 1913; 3; *Daily News*, April 8, 1913: 1.

The exact number of victims who perished at the Idlewild Club is unknown. Other accounts say twenty-five men died there, but I could find evidence of only nineteen confirmed deaths of people who were in the club when the tornado struck.

2. *Omaha Daily Bee*, March 24, 1913: 3.

3. *Omaha Daily News*, March 24, 1913: 9.

4. *Omaha Daily Bee*, March 26, 1913: 6.

5. *Omaha Daily Bee*, March 25, 1913: 3.

6. *Omaha Daily News*, March 26, 1913: 4.

7. *Omaha Excelsior*, March 29, 1913: 11.

8. Ibid.

9. *Daily News*, March 24, 1913: 3.

10. Ibid.

11. *Excelsior*, March 29, 1913.

12. *Bee*, March 26, 1913: 13; *Omaha Daily News*, March 29, 1913: 2.

13. *Excelsior*, March 29, 1913.

14. *Bee*, March 24, 1913: 4.

15. *Bee*, March 26, 1913: 9.

16. Ibid.

17. *Omaha Daily News*, April 19, 1913: 1.

18. Jens Jensen File (Archives of Joslyn Castle Institute for Sustainable Communities).

19. *Omaha Daily News*, October 12, 1913: 5C.

20. *Omaha World-Herald* (Evening Edition), October 17, 1913: 12.

21. Ibid.

22. *Omaha Excelsior*, October 18, 1913: 11.

23. *Omaha Daily Bee*, October 17, 1913: 8.

The account in the *Bee* mentions that the bridal table was decorated with President Taft Roses. While I assume this means they were a gift from President Taft, the referral might also be to a type of rose. However, I could find no record of any species of rose being identified as a "President Taft."

24. *Excelsior*, 11.

25. *World-Herald*, 12.

26. *Omaha Daily News*, October 17, 1913: 12.

27. *Excelsior*, 11.

28. *Omaha Excelsior*, August 22, 1914: 12.

29. *New York Times*, January 18, 1914: 1.

30. *Omaha Daily News*, January 28, 1914: 1.

31. *Omaha Daily Bee*, January 28, 1914: 2.

32. UNO Alumni Association, "Birth of Joslyn Hall" (2004), http://www.unoalumni.org/ About_Us/Flashback/Archive/109/index.asp (April 8, 2005).

33. George Joslyn dedication speech (Archives of Joslyn Castle Institute for Sustainable Communities).

34. Ibid.

35. Ibid.

36. *Omaha Excelsior*, July 4, 1914: 2.

37. *Omaha Daily News*, October 4, 1916: 1.

38. *Omaha Excelsior*, March 20, 1915: 4.

39. *1914 Omaha City Directory.*

40. *Omaha Excelsior*, April 24, 1915: 11; *Excelsior*, September 4, 1915: 13.

The *Omaha Excelsior* carried an article in its April 24, 1915 issue telling of the Joslyns' plans. The paper continued to list them at that address each week until early September.

41. *Omaha Daily Bee*, September 16, 1916: 1.

42. *Omaha Excelsior*, February 12, 1916: 4.

43. *Omaha Excelsior*, February 19, 1916: 2.

44. *Omaha Daily News*, October 4, 1916: 1, 3.

45. *Omaha World-Herald*, October 7, 1916: 6.

46. Ibid.

47. Joslyn dedication speech.

Chapter Nine:

1. *Omaha Excelsior*, April 7, 1917: 14.

2. *Omaha Daily News*, November 1, 1917: 10.

3. *Omaha Excelsior*, September 8, 1917: 11.

4. *Omaha Excelsior*, April 6, 1918: 14.

5. *Omaha Excelsior*, January 12, 1918: 13.

6. *Omaha Excelsior*, January 26, 1918: 11.

7. *Omaha Excelsior*, March 9, 1918: 11.

8. *Omaha World-Herald*, September 6, 1918: 3.

9. *Omaha World-Herald*, September 23, 1917: 8.

10. Ibid.

11. *Omaha Excelsior*, September 7, 1918: 4.

12. Ibid.

13. *Omaha Excelsior*, February 8, 1919: 4.

14. Emporis Buildings, "Medical Arts Building, Omaha" (2004), http://www.emporis.com/en/wm/bu/?id=102896 (March 27, 2005).

15. *Omaha Excelsior*, April 24, 1920: 4.

16. *Omaha Daily News*, February 28, 1914: 1.

17. *Omaha Daily News*, March 15, 1914: 3C.

18. *Omaha Daily News*, May 12, 1914: 1.

19. *Omaha Excelsior*, May 30, 1914: 5.

20. *Daily News*, 1.

21. *Omaha Excelsior*, January 25, 1919: 4.

22. *Omaha Excelsior*, May 1, 1920: 4.

23. *Omaha Excelsior*, October 2, 1920: 1.

24. *Omaha Daily News*, October 8, 1920: 6.

25. *Omaha Daily News*, December 27, 1922: 1–2.

26. Ibid.

27. Ibid.

28. Ibid.

29. *Omaha World-Herald*, December 28, 1922: 1.

30. *Daily News*, 2.

31. Ibid.

32. *Omaha World-Herald*, February 28, 1940: 10.

33. *Omaha World-Herald*, May 6, 1928: 1.

34. *New York Times*, July 3, 1929: 11.

35. *Omaha Excelsior*, October 23, 1920: 6.

36. *Omaha World-Herald*, March 15, 1940: 9.

37. *Omaha World-Herald*, November 30, 1931: 1.

38. Ibid.

Chapter Ten:

1. Transcript, Sally Hersey and Joslyn Birdzell, Oral History Interview, September 26, 1991, by Audrey Kauders, Elizabeth Garrison, Ruby Hagerbaumer, and Lannie McNichols (Archives of the Joslyn Castle Institute for Sustainable Communities).

2. *Omaha World-Herald*, April 24, 1934: 1.

3. Ibid.

4. Ibid.

5. Ibid.

6. *New York Times*, April 24, 1940: 4.

7. *World-Herald*, 1.

8. *Omaha World-Herald*, February 28, 1940: 1, 10.

9. Ibid.

10. Ibid.

11. Graham W. J. Beale, *Joslyn Art Museum: A Building History* (Joslyn Art Museum, 1994): 13.

12. *Omaha World-Herald*, February 29, 1940: 1, 10.

13. *Omaha World-Herald*, March 5, 1940: 1, 6.

14. Ibid.

15. *Omaha Daily News*, June 13, 1917: 4.

16. *Omaha Excelsior*, November 2, 1907: 3.

Epilogue:

1. *New York Times*, April 14, 1952: 29.

2. LDS search: Violet Magowan (August 4, 2005).

3. LDS search: David Magowan (August 4, 2005).

4. *New York Times*, January 17, 1946: 17.

5. LDS search: Sally Hersey (August 4, 2005).

6. *New York Times*, May 9, 1943: 38.

7. *Omaha World-Herald*, December 30, 2005: 4B.

8. Transcript, Miss Anne Traub, Oral History Interview, August 9, 1944, by Omaha Public Schools (Archives of the Joslyn Castle Institute for Sustainable Communities).

9. *Omaha Excelsior*, December 8, 1917: 14.

10. Diane E. Stiles et al., "Hollywood Forever Cemetery: Los Angles County, California" (Surnames A–F), http://www.interment.net/data/us/ca/losangeles/hollywood/hollywood_af.htm (August 4, 2005).

The name listed in the surnames index is Nettie A. Bidwell, not Hattie, and Hattie Bidwell's middle initial was *S*, so it is still close to Mrs. Bidwell's name. In addition, the birth year is the same as Hattie's; therefore, this may or may not be Hattie.

11. FLCA: R, http://www.forestlawnomaha.com/GraveIndex/IndexSummaryR.html (August 4, 2005).

12. *New York Times*, February 11, 1950: 12.

13. *New York Times*, July 16, 1952: 25.

14. *Omaha City Directory,* 1904 through 1906.

15. This information was contained in a letter to the author from the Society of American Florists.

16. FLCA: M, http://www.forestlawnomaha.com/GraveIndex/IndexSummaryM.html (August 4, 2005).

17. City of Omaha Landmarks Heritage Preservation Commission, "John McDonald," http://www.ci.omaha.ne.us/landmarks/designated_landmarks/architects/McDonald.htm (August 4, 2005).

18. Graham W. J. Beale, *Joslyn Art Museum: A Building History* (Joslyn Art Museum, 1994): 78, 98.

19. *Omaha World-Herald*, November 30, 1931: 1.

Index

A

Aeolian 62, 63, 79, 86, 96, 97, 122, 132, 147, 149, 150
Aeolian Organ Company 97
Aeolus 63
Aluminum Leaf 61
American Guild of Organists 97
American Press Association 6, 108
Anderson, Margaret 113
Andrews, Walter E. 4
Arcade Hotel 10, 13
Art Institute of Omaha 119
Art-Glass ix, 51, 62, 63, 64, 66, 67, 70, 76, 77, 78, 79, 80, 82, 85
Association of Commercial Clubs of the Pacific Coast 98
Auxiliary Printing Industry 3, 4, 5, 6

B

Bach, Martin 64
Baldridge, Howard 104
Baldridge, Mrs. Howard 104
Baldwin, John N. 88
Bangs and Whiton School 102
Barrault, Harry 24
Bartizan 32, 44
Baxter, William F. 136
Bay Chief 22, 29, 36
Beach, Moses 4

Bidwell, George 13, 14, 102, 135
Bidwell, Hattie 13, 28, 107, 158
Big G xii, 137
Birdzell, Joslyn Magowan 10
Birdzell, Luther 135
Block, Maurice 116
Boilerplate 5
Boyce, Angie 11
Boyce, Eugene 11, 141
Brain, John 11
Brick Presbyterian Church 97
Brownell Academy 27, 101
Bryan, William Jennings 87, 101
Buffalo Bill 100
Burgess, Mrs. Ward 116

C

Calfas, Dr. Jennie 113
Camp Bord du Lac 14, 94
Carl, Violet 26, 27
Carpenter, Charles G. 19, 135
Carriage House 26, 28, 29, 30, 32, 37, 41, 48
Chamberlain, Betsy 1
Chase, Clement 94, 135
Chase, Clement and Lula Belle 13
Chase, Lula Belle 13, 26, 65, 101, 115
Chicago & Northwestern Railroad 14
Child Saving Institute 108, 113
Christian, Palmer 120

City Beautiful 17
Cody, Colonel William F. 100
Columbian Exposition 16, 17, 19, 51, 52, 66, 143
Cook Remedy Company xii, 10
Corbelling 32, 42
Corbie Gable 32, 44
Corning, Erastus 24
Cowboy Line 13
Cowin, General John C. 108
Crenellation 32
Crummer, Dr. Le Roy 110
Currier & Ives 29

D

Daniels, Cliff 104
Davis, Alexander Jackson 15
Davis, Elizabeth 102
Dentil Molding 63
Dietz, Gould 100, 132
Dietz, Leonora 132
Dietz, Mrs. Gould 100
Drum Turret 32, 42

E

Edison, Thomas Alva 99
Egg-and-Dart 60, 61
Evans Chemical Company xii, 137

F

F. Sander Company 24
Fang, Minister Wu Ting 26
Farnsworth, Angie 135
Farnsworth, Coit 118, 135
Ferguson, Judge Arthur N. 16
First Unitarian Church 132, 133
Fish, Herbert H. 110
Flanagan, Father Edward 132
Fleming, Omer 132
Fleming, William 89, 92

Flicker, Hannah 133
Flower Parade 26, 35
FOJC ix
Forest Lawn Cemetery 10, 13, 64, 111, 135, 140, 141
Frank, Fritz 131
Friends of Joslyn Castle vii, ix, 39, 47, 48, 49, 53, 55, 57, 58, 60, 72, 73, 75, 126, 127, 136
Fusionists 87

G

Gardenesque 15, 19
George and Sarah ix, xi, 1, 2, 4, 8, 9, 10, 11, 12, 13, 14, 15, 17, 22, 23, 25, 27, 28, 29, 30, 31, 36, 38, 51, 62, 64, 67, 68, 89, 90, 93, 94, 96, 97, 98, 101, 103, 107, 108, 109, 110, 134, 146
Gibson, Archer 96, 97, 103, 122, 135
Gibson, S. Archer 96, 97, 122
Ginkgo 20, 21, 144
Gleason, Mary Wallis 10
Gordon, John C. 134
Grand Union Hotel 93
Grummann, Dr. Paul 119

H

Hall, Matthew 104
Haller, Frank 101
Haller, Mrs. F. L. 100
Harp of Aeolus 63
Herbert, Victor 63
Hersey, John 135
Hersey, Sally Magowan 10
Hinton, Carmelita 135
Hoar, John 9
Hogg, Maude 104
Horticultural Building 18
Hotel Hollywood 110
Hotel Imperial 17, 51
Hotel Joslyn 9

I

Idlewild Club 103, 151
Iowa Printing Company 4

J

Jacobean 66, 83
Jensen, Jens 18, 143, 152
Jones, Herbert D. 11
Joseph Joslin Memorial Library Building 109
Joslin, Alfred 2, 138
Joslin, Almon 9
Joslin, Ferdinand 140
Joslin, Frederick Abner 10
Joslin, Jennie 141
Joslin, Joseph 1, 109, 111, 133, 137, 138
Joslyn Castle vii, ix, 15, 18, 21, 31, 32, 39, 47, 48,
   49, 51, 53, 55, 57, 58, 60, 72, 73, 75, 80, 126,
   127, 136, 137, 140, 141, 145, 147, 151, 152,
   156, 157
Joslyn Castle Institute vii, 136, 137, 140, 141, 145,
   151, 152, 156, 157
Joslyn Hall 108, 153
Joslyn Memorial 13, 26, 63, 115, 119, 130, 133,
   134
Joslyn Memorial Art Museum 13, 115
Joslyn, George 3, 4, 16, 97, 110, 119, 138
Joslyn, George Alfred 40
Joslyn, Sarah ix, xii, 8, 10, 34, 75, 89, 107, 115,
   133, 134, 141
Joslyn, Violet 27, 106
Jungten, Mrs. Mary 98

K

Kiplinger, Gladys 16
Krinski, Nathan 104

L

Lake Saratoga 14, 36, 94
Leavens, Reverend Robert 110
Limestone 21, 32

Lincrusta 67
Lindbergh Law 132
Linden Glass Company 51, 63, 78
Line Corporation 89
Lininger Art Gallery 100
Lininger, George W. 115
Little White Rose 63
Lyman, Dr. Harry 98
Lyman, Mr. and Mrs. Charles 98
Lyndhurst vii, 15, 24, 142
Lyndhurst on the Hudson vii
Lynhurst xi, 13, 14, 15, 16, 18, 19, 20, 21, 22, 23,
   28, 31, 32, 39, 40, 42, 45, 50, 51, 52, 62, 85, 87,
   90, 94, 97, 98, 100, 101, 102, 103, 104, 105,
   106, 110, 113, 114, 118, 119, 120, 121, 123,
   128, 130, 132, 133, 135, 136
Lynhurst Castle 42, 45, 51, 52, 85, 128
Lynhurst Estate 94, 133
Lyte, Thomas 106

M

MacKay, Reverend Thomas 110
Mad River Valley 1
Magowan, David 102, 106, 107, 113, 157
Maney Bond 22
Matsubara, Kazuo 99
McAllister, Ziba 108
McDonald, Alan 102, 117, 118, 135
McDonald, John 12, 31, 51, 102, 109, 118, 119,
   135, 142, 158
McHenry, Frank 11
McKinley, President William 26
Metropolitan Hotel 8, 9, 12
Mickey, Governor John H. 88
Midzuno, Kokichi 99
Millard, Jessie 100
Mines and Mining Building 26
Modjeska 65
Modjeska, Madame Helena 65

Morehead, Governor John H. 105
Muffitt, Edward 132

N

National Humane Society 113
National League of Women's Services 113
Nebraska Building 19, 66
Nebraska State Equalization Board 89
Nebraska Supreme Court 16
Nebraska's Twenty-Eighth Legislature 87
Northwestern Newspaper Union 6

O

Ogilevy, David 12
Old People's Home 109, 110, 133, 134
Omaha Association for the Protection of Boys and
  Girls 113
Omaha Bee 33, 94, 123, 142
Omaha City Council 94
Omaha Country Club 90, 101
Omaha Daily News 90, 94, 109, 117, 121, 143, 145,
  147, 148, 150, 151, 152, 153, 154, 155, 157
Omaha Excelsior 9, 13, 20, 28, 38, 94, 98, 116, 122,
  134, 139, 140, 141, 142, 143, 144, 146, 147,
  148, 149, 150, 151, 152, 153, 154, 155, 156, 157
Omaha Newspaper Union 4, 6
Omaha Public Library vii, 34, 35, 115, 140
Omaha Public School System 20, 21, 86
Omaha Real Estate Board 94
Omaha School Supply Company 11
Omaha Society of Fine Arts 117, 119
Omaha University 108, 132, 133
Omaha World-Herald vii, 19, 20, 30, 94, 119, 133,
  137, 138, 140, 142, 143, 144, 146, 148, 149,
  152, 154, 155, 156, 157, 158
OPS 21, 136
Opus 1035 62
Orchids 23, 24, 25, 105, 107
Our Magic Remedy xii

P

Patterson Building 109, 110, 118
Pianola 62
Pickens, Charles 104
Picturesque 15, 17, 19, 31, 32, 49, 50
Picturesque Revival 31, 32
Pipal, Frank 20
Populists 87, 88
Prairie School 18, 63

Q

Quezal 64, 148

R

Railroad Lobby 88
Ready Print 5
Redick, William 13, 28, 135
Reisdorff, Joseph 113
Rice, Ester Ann 2
Roman, Isaac 25, 47, 90, 123
Rosewater, Edward 94
Russell, Charles W. 119
Russell, Fremont M. 66

S

Safford 38, 65
Saint-Saens, Camille 63
Samuels, Chief John M. 18
Schlitz Building 109
Schlitz European Hotel 109
Scobie, Helen 102
Scott, Walter W. 123
Scottish Baronial ix, 30, 31, 32, 41, 43, 52, 63, 67,
  147
Search Light 29, 36
Selleck, James 1
Selleck, Lucelia 141
Selleck, Sarah Hannah 2
Shibusawa Ei'ichi Memorial Foundation 99, 150

Shibusawa, Baron 99, 100, 101
Shibusawa, Baroness 100
Simms, Frank 96
Smith, Courtland 108
Society of American Florists 135, 158
Society of Liberal Arts 13, 118, 119, 135, 136
Spence, William M. 11
Spierling & Linden 51, 52
St. Charles Hotel 9, 10
Stanley, Ben 106, 110
Starkey, Rose Matilda (Tillie) 9
State Printing Company 4
Stereotype 5, 6
Sunday, Reverend Billy 110
Sutphen, Clinton Joy 16
Sutton, Judge Abraham L. 16

T
Taft, Frank 96
Taft, Helen 99
Taft, President William Howard 99, 107
Taylor, Abigail 2, 138
Technical High School 136
Thorpe, John 18, 19, 135
Tilden, Ida 109
Tobitt, Edith 115, 117, 118
Tornado 98, 103, 104, 105, 123, 125, 151
Toyo 66
Trans-Mississippi Exposition 14, 19, 22, 25, 26, 34, 35
Tufa 21, 60
Turner Mansion 115
Twenty-Eighth Legislature 87, 88, 89

U
Ulrich, Rudolf 19
Union Pacific Railroad 88, 100
Updike, Nelson 105

V
Veitch & Sons 24
Vermont 1, 2, 4, 9, 10, 11, 64, 138
Visiting Nurse Association 20, 133

W
Wait, General Benjamin 1
Waitsfield, Vermont 1, 138
Want-A-Teepee 14
Ward, Dr. Nathaniel Bagshaw 24
Washington County 1, 138
Washington, Alfred 108
Watson, Elmo Scott 6
Wattles, Gurdon 14, 107
Webster, John L. 116
Welsh, William H. 4
Western Art Association 115
Western Newspaper Union 6, 8, 9, 89, 91, 92, 107, 108, 116, 135
White City 17, 18
Wilson, Mrs. George B. 24
WNU 6, 8, 9, 10, 12, 14, 89, 108, 109, 110, 119
Wright, Frank Lloyd 63, 78, 147

Y
Ye, Minister Chin Pom 26
Yost, Casper 98

978-0-595-38576-8
0-595-38576-1